THE BACHELOR'S GUIDE TO FIRST DATE COOKING

Whether you're a kitchen novice or a seasoned pro,
this is your step-by-step blueprint on how to achieve
top-chef prowess on the first date — and beyond!

CHRIS DE LUCA

DEDICATION

This project is dedicated to my family and friends, who are constant
and unwavering.

I also dedicate this project to my dog, Charlie.
On December 3, 2001 – his special day – Charlie came home with me
from the Humane Society.
He's been the ultimate wingman ever since.
Thank you, Charlie, for many years of devout loyalty.

"The Big Looch"

ACKNOWLEDGEMENTS

I would like to thank the following people for assisting me in the creation of this book:

Thomas Hauck – Thank you for your insightful editorial skill. Without your help this could not have happened.

Erin Wilkinson – Thank you for your patience and wisdom in coordinating all of the tasks that I just could not do.

Deborah Cull Photography

Andrijana Filipovic

Debra Bryan

The Lucarelli Family

Kate Piscatori Zeto

Chef Omar Hafidi – Thank you for teaching me concept in the kitchen. Your lessons live on in every facet of my life.

CONTENTS

LOCAL CHILDREN'S CHARITY

A percentage of the proceeds from every sale of this book will go to a Southern Florida children's charity that grants the wishes of children with life-threatening conditions. This local children's charity enriches the human experience with hope, strength and joy.

Donating is an easy decision for me, having seen firsthand the amazing results. In 2008 my cousin's son, Cody Snelling, was stricken with cancer. Cody was only twelve years old at the time. As a result of the disease, Cody had his leg amputated at the knee. How does a healthy, active child go from playing little league baseball to fighting for his life?

Cancer is ruthless and unbiased, and seems even crueler when it strikes a child. In Cody's greatest hour of need, this children's charity stepped in and granted Cody his wish of a Caribbean vacation for him and his family. Today, Cody is strong and still fighting, and I can't help but think the power of positive outlook was instrumental in strengthening his will to fight. It makes you realize that good things *do* happen, in turn giving you the will to persevere.

The mind is a powerful thing. A person's optimistic outlook can give the power to overcome challenges that would otherwise be insurmountable. A person always finds a way to see something through when they have optimism and the belief that they can. Belief and optimism are so very important for anyone to have, especially a child.

If you could bring this power to a child suffering from a life-threatening condition by taking part in granting their wish, I'm sure it would be an easy decision for you as well. So please get involved. Donate. Help out. I reach out to you to do it somewhere. Help a child with a life-threatening condition realize their dream.

For more information on how to get involved, please visit this web site - www.sfla.wish.org

Thank you for your support.

PREFACE

In today's dating world, you need to play to win. There's so much to consider when selecting a potential mate. As you negotiate your way through the dating maze, you're going to find that one thing always holds true: the laws of natural selection. They are ruthless and will cause you to succeed or fail in many ways. These laws govern every aspect of who you are and how women perceive you.

First impressions are important. At first impression, women will always judge men by their appearance. A well-dressed, good looking, confident man always has a leg up.

A man's income is always going to be a concern. Who can blame her for wanting to associate with a successful guy? A comfortable home or apartment, financial stability, a guy who's happy to pay the restaurant bill or bar tab, a good provider for the family, you can't blame her for wanting these things, it's only natural.

A sense of humor helps; every woman likes to laugh. No woman wants a rigid, no-fun guy. As important as it is to be financially secure, it's equally important to have balance between making money and enjoying the fruits of your labor. Besides, why should you be making all of the money and she's the only person enjoying it?

You know that you're in an ultra-competitive dating market. There's a bunch of good-looking, successful, funny, charismatic guys out there. Sure, you're good looking. Sure, you're successful. Sure, you're laugh-out-loud funny. So what's going to set you apart from the rest of the pack?

What will change your dating landscape are the secrets in this book. My strategy will help you go from dating purgatory to having more dating opportunities than you know what to do with. These concepts, ideas, and tools will help you elevate your social life into a robust and full experience.

What is it? Very simple:

Planning, preparing, and executing the perfect first date culinary experience.

Every woman loves a renaissance man. The man who can bring home the bacon and then fry it up is a valuable commodity. The fact is that today's women are more apt to have full-time careers and are less apt to be domestic. The man who can cook is going to have many, many advantages in today's dating world. I've done a lot of dating, and I've found that there's no better first date than to treat her to an intimate evening of dinner for two, or afternoon by the pool, or night on the couch, with some great food and fun.

Think about it. The conversation pieces, the intimacy of sharing a dinner for two, the opportunity for one-on-one time without distractions, the chance to drink wine, the chance to share in the process of cooking, and showing a woman you're not helpless in the kitchen but fearless. These examples all add up to one thing: more and better dates.

While writing *The Bachelor's Guide to First Date Cooking*, it became clear to me what this book really is. It's a how-to book. My book is a "how – to" that combines two vital bachelor skills: cooking and dating. I'm going to teach you how to combine a "soft" skill like cooking with the masculine task of asking a woman out. Cooking and dating come together perfectly. You will learn that when the two are combined, it's a natural fit.

But more importantly, it's a how-to on getting out of your own way. All too often we get in our own way. We make excuses, posture, close down and get nervous, and don't know what to say or how to say it.

Would this behavior produce results in the workplace? No way. And it won't produce results on the dating scene either.

You need a plan. You need a simple, well thought-out plan. Nothing contrived, but an easy way to approach a girl and say hello…something with a little purpose. The idea isn't to manipulate or deceive, but to give you a better opportunity to meet a girl. Because the true goal is to find the girl who not only inspires you, but does it with a feeling of comfort and contentment.

Attraction without pretense is the strategy. More and better dates for you is the goal. And you can achieve this… just like I have.

I'll get you through the door and get you started on your first date. I'll make it easy, I promise.

Enjoy and happy first dating.

Chris

INTRODUCTION

The most important thing you should know about cooking is summed up in one simple quote: "*It took Picasso an entire lifetime to learn how to paint like a child.*" Keep it simple. A lot of steps in a recipe do not necessarily make the dish better. Genius is in simplicity. The simpler you keep it; the less likely you are to mess it up.

If I wanted to teach you math for the first time, I wouldn't give you a calculus book. I'd start with the basics. Walk before you run. The food and preparations in this book are fun and easy. And when presented on the table, these recipes have the appearance of taking refined skill to prepare. But here's the truth: if you can boil water and cut with a knife, you can create delicious and memorable meals that will set you apart from the crowd.

I'll show you that if you stick to a few key ingredients you can cook almost anything. Whether your main protein is red meat, poultry, fish, shellfish, game fowl, or pork, these key ingredients will complement each other and your dish will always come out tasting good. The key ingredients are:

- Tomatoes
- Garlic
- Olive oil
- Fresh herbs
- Wine
- Fresh vegetables – zucchini, yellow squash, eggplant, peppers.
- Salt and fresh cracked pepper

All of these foods are readily available and easy to work with. They will also look amazing when they are sliced, diced, julienned, and spread out across your counter top. Very impressive when she walks in and sees these beautiful foods organized and ready to be assembled. She'll think she's walking onto the set of a cooking show. Of course you will have to leave a little work for her to see you actually do some of this, but that's the fun – looking top-chef nasty.

As we go along through the book, if you don't know what something is or how to say it, be patient. I'll explain it to you. I'm good at that. You will find that behind all of the fancy French culinary terms for food and preparation lays an easy explanation of what it means. That's why I'm writing this book. If I had a nickel for every one of my friends that I had to explain what something is or how to cook it, I'd have a lot of nickels.

If you don't find the meaning in the text, I'm sure you will find it in the glossary or on my website. The website is designed to be interactive. All of the *fancy-schmancy* culinary terms and *fancy-schmancy* French words are hyperlinked to give you the meaning immediately. The website will also have a two- to three-minute demonstration of every dish – soup to nuts – from the beginning ingredients, to preparation, to the finished product. To see is to learn, at least for most of us guys. And if you don't find the information that you're looking for? Drop me an email. I'll get back to you. I promise.

To make it as easy as possible, you'll see that throughout the book are bullet-point lists. When you see a list marked with little circles, like this:

- Item 1
- Item 2
- Item 3

It means that these are items – food or utensils – you will need to buy and have in your kitchen. Just like the list above.

Even if you have never cooked before, or if your idea of "cooking" has been to put a container of processed frozen glop into the microwave, you can take control of your culinary life and use it to improve your dating life. You can apply the same discipline that you have at the workplace or on the golf course and transfer it to the kitchen. We're going to take that simple chicken breast and turn it into a masterpiece. We're going to take an ordinary head of lettuce and turn it into a work of art. *The Bachelor's Guide to First Date Cooking* will serve as your first date "go-to" information book. You will learn how to slice, dice, julienne, and flambé like a top chef. Or at least you'll have the confidence of one.

Let's get started!

CHAPTER 1: THE PLATFORM

"With the privilege of being able to date often comes the responsibility of not being a scumbag about it. Be honest. Be forthright. Give her the chance to make decisions based on facts and not deceit. And if your intentions are to go out, have a great time, laugh? There's no harm in that."

LET'S TAKE A MOMENT and define the term "player." With the MTV generation and the reality TV shows, the word player adorns many young men and women as a badge of honor. If you're a player, you have the ability to attract and date numerous people as if it were a game.

Let's talk about this from the young adult single male's perspective. I'm referring to the guy who's intelligent, responsible, and on the right path in life. This young adult makes informative life decisions that distinguish him as mature from the immature. Now, throw into that equation the ability to date often. Question – if a man makes the decision to stay single and date, does this make him a bad guy? I don't think so.

It takes pioneers – renegades – to have the courage to be single and date versus getting married for the wrong reasons. Because the rules of the mainstream telling us we have to get married is no reason to do so. I'm a firm believer in being in a committed relationship with someone you love and trust. However, what I'm not a believer in is getting married because this is what the world is telling us to do. Ultimately, only you can live your life. It's going to be you who see in the mirror every day.

Don't take this out of context. If you love someone and want to spend the rest of your life with that someone, then get married. All I'm saying is do it for the right reasons. It's a fact that today's divorce rate is upwards of 50%. The bottom line is that times are very different for us than for our parents.

The man who makes the choice to be single and date responsibly is not a bad person. It only becomes bad if he does this under false pretense, deception and lying. Taking responsibility and saying, "You know something, I date, I date often, and that's why I'm single," is OK. This is a conscious choice you have the right to make. A man who is forthright about this is not a bad guy. Who's the bad guy here, the married man who cheats on his wife or the single guy who dates and doesn't lie about it?

∾ "THIRTY-SOMETHING" IS THE NEW TWENTY ∾

We have become bigger, faster, and stronger, and are able to maintain this far longer. Talk of thirty-something being the new 20? It's true. I'm 38 years old and feel better, look better, and perform better than when I was 22.

It's fact that a man's window of opportunity to date is left open far longer than in years past. Let's take a look at how men have evolved over the past 30 years. In the NFL, it was rare to see lineman who broke 300 lbs and still had athletic ability. Today, linemen are 6'2", weigh 325 lbs, and can run the 40 in less than five seconds.

In the early 1990s, power forwards like Karl Malone and Larry Johnson were freaks at 6'8" and 250 lbs. Today, there are guys like Lebron James who are 6'8", 275 lbs, and possess speed and agility far superior to players much smaller.

There's so much new information and advances in staying healthy that today's *thirty-something* man often has the appearance of being in his twenties. Men well into their 30s and even 40s can date considerably longer with the appearance of nothing out of place. So, what's wrong with this? If you're not hurting anyone, what's the problem?

If a man has the social skills to function in an adult environment and is being emotionally mature to handle relationship's challenges, what's wrong with him being single and dating? If someone gives you a Ferrari with a full tank of gas, do you leave it in the garage? You drive it like you're Magnum PI in Hawaii. If genetics gives you the ability to date young attractive women, do you not do it? You date and you date often.

∽ WITH CONFIDENCE COMES RESPONSIBILITY ∽

But you need to uphold a social contract. With the privilege of being able to date often comes the responsibility of not being a scumbag about it. Be honest. Be forthright. Give her the chance to make decisions based on facts and not deceit. And if your intentions are to go out, have a great time, laugh? There's no harm in that.

It's only perceived to be "wrong" because maybe she wants a little more out of the potential relationship and she then throws out the word player as a matter of spite. The reality – she's only doing this because maybe she wants what you don't want right now.

Everyone knows what has happened to Tiger Woods. He made some serious mistakes. You don't do the things he did as a married man. However, I think that his biggest mistake was getting married in the first place. Perhaps a person in his position should never have gotten married. People make mistakes. However, he clearly was not ready to be in a committed relationship. Maybe the appearance of a wife and children was good for business in his eyes. "Good for business" or "Keep up appearances" are reasons to get married – but not the *right* ones. If he had remained single, he would've been a billionaire good-looking professional athlete with the ability to date and one who happens to act on it. Whether you agree with that or not is OK. But if he were single, things would be very different for him right now.

Being a single man by choice takes confidence. Being a single man by choice takes truly being happy with you. It takes more courage to do what makes you truly happy versus what people think you're supposed to do. What may be happiness for some may not be for others. Only you can determine your own path to happiness. It's always the person considered the pioneer, the trendsetter, the innovator, or the genius who decides to take the road less traveled.

Remember, critics are cynics. Cynics are the ones that don't have ability, so they criticize. Let them say what they want. Judgment is reserved for two people: the man in the mirror, and the man above. And before anyone can judge, they need to walk a mile. I wonder how the cynics would react if beautiful women were throwing themselves at them. I wonder what kind of self-control they would have.

Be happy. Do what makes you happy. And stick to your guns. Or, get married because everyone thinks you should. What the hell, you got a 50/50 shot right?

CHAPTER 2: THE FIRST DATE BLUEPRINT

"I've seen a lot of good-looking guys who always have trouble with women. The reality is that once you're outside of the nightclub, genuine social skills come in handy when you have to talk to her instead of yelling in her ear."

LET'S DISCUSS the tools you'll need to execute the perfect home-cooked first date. I'll outline the tools, cutlery, cookware, glassware, and all of that stuff. But first, let's talk about the skills that will make the first encounter that much easier. Let's face it – 99 times out of 100, when a woman catches your eye, you're going to stand there and do nothing. You're going to posture, try to look cool, and hope she sends her friend over, or give you the "OK" signal to approach.

I'm going to show you how to take the pressure off. I will teach you what to say, how to say it, and how to initialize it. I'll give you some psychological tools that will help.

∾ PRESENCE ∾

It's human nature for a woman to be attracted to a man's appearance. If you're a good-looking guy it helps. However, looks will only get you so far. I've seen a lot of good-looking guys who always have trouble with women. The reality is that once you're outside of the nightclub, genuine social skills come in handy when you have to talk to her instead of yelling in her ear.

We'll start with the most valuable characteristic a man can have in the single world: *presence.* Some people just have it. Presence means you walk into the room and people know you've arrived. It's innate. Presence is made up of five different characteristics:

1. Confidence
2. Character
3. Posture
4. Appearance
5. Attitude

Confidence means have some balls, plain and simple. Be bold. The world rewards the bold. The truth is that guys who won't approach a woman hold back because they're afraid of rejection. Guys will say, "I don't wanna be that guy," or "Only cheesy guys do that," or "I'll let her come to me." OK there, cool guy.

Character means having principles and sticking to your guns. Whatever they may be, stick to them no matter what. But don't mistake this with pride. Pride can sometimes be foolish. It can stand in your way between dating a fantastic woman and being too cool to approach her.

Your mother used to tell you to stand up straight. Guess what? Ma was right. A man's **posture** tells a lot. This is very simple. Don't slouch – you'll look like a loser. Be confident. Walk tall. That's why the military drills this into soldiers.

Your **appearance** tells the story of who you are and what a girl can expect. Look good, feel good, and sound good. When you look sharp and you know it, the better you're going to feel. When you're feeling good, the more confident you're going to sound. And when you're sounding confident, it's on. Whenever I would plan a get-together at my place, I would bill the party as semi-formal. When people were dressed a little more formally, I would notice that their behavior would follow suit. People would be shaking hands, meeting and greeting, and having fun.

How a person dresses directly affects their behavior. That's why you dress business formal for work. When you're dressed professional, you act professional. Find your own style sense. Don't let your ex-girlfriend dress you. One of two things happen – you feel like you're wearing a costume, or she told you that skinny jeans look sexy. Yes, most women have good fashion sense, but they are women. If you have a football team, you don't hire a basketball coach.

The truth is we are all not Calvin Klein models. Not all of us can get away with low-rise Italian jeans and fitted v-neck tee shirts. We're also not train wrecks either.

Remember, all magazine pictures are done by a professional photographer for a reason, and that's to hide flaws. All department and boutique clothing stores elongate their mirrors and set the lighting perfectly to make you look taller and skinny. They're in business and they're trying to sell you. No one's perfect. All you can do is find what's perfect for you.

Everything that I just talked about – confidence, character, posture, and appearance – all combine to form **attitude.** When I say attitude, I'm referring to your disposition or feeling towards something. A person's attitude is quite simply their outlook on life. The mind is a powerful thing. It can make you happy, sad, upset, or frustrated. The good news is that social maturity is defined by taking responsibility for how you feel. You can't control what people do or say, but you CAN control how you let it (or don't let it) affect you.

If "attitude" is defined as your outlook, make it a positive one. You have the ability to do this. That's what I'm talking about when I say that successful people have short-term negative memory. Did she turn you down? Forget about it, keep smiling, and move on. Project a positive attitude. It's true – attitude is everything.

If you are unhappy (your boss is a jerk or your girlfriend just dumped you), you can start to change how you feel inside by changing the outside. You may be feeling totally sorry for yourself, but acting with a positive attitude can transform how you feel. If you make these key behaviors part of your everyday life, you can attain an inviting, friendly, positive attitude in a social setting – whether a bar, nightclub, happy hour, or even back at your place in the kitchen.

1. **Smile**. A smile is the best way to let the world view you. If you have to force it at first, that's OK. Eventually you won't, because something as easy as smiling will yield great results, and make you smile anyway.

2. **Say "Hello."** When you make eye contact with someone, say hello. It's friendly. It's polite. It sets the tone for the rest of the night. Heaven forbid you should say "hello" and meet a new friend!

3. **Dance.** Take a lesson from McLovin in the movie *Superbad*. Women love to dance. And the secret to being a great dancer? The best dance move I know? Easy…it's not caring how you look, and having fun. Don't sit on the sidelines making fun of the guys dancing. Guess what – they're out dancing with the pretty girls, and you're on the sidelines with all the cynics who will go home alone. Don't be a cynic.

4. **Confidence!** The one with the most confidence is the one that isn't afraid to be a little goofy and have fun. This doesn't mean be the class clown, but have the ability to laugh at yourself. Again, don't be the guy on the sideline making fun or criticizing. Remember, you're in the game, and they're on the sidelines. I would much rather play than ride the benches.

Anyone can do these things. Be positive. Think positive. Positive attitude breeds positive results, especially in the mission to approach a woman.

∾ GET OVER YOURSELF ∾

Everyone is afraid of rejection. And don't tell me you've never been turned down. Yeah, right. The reason is you never take a chance and approach someone that hasn't given you a signal first. There are always women you're attracted to, but they haven't given you the green light. When you wait for the girl to make the first move, it's called the path of least resistance, and this leads to mediocrity.

◦◦ THE APPROACH ◦◦

Look, we all know that not everyone is going to like you. It's the simple rule that you can't please everyone all of the time. It's fact. So, please listen carefully and take this to heart. When it comes to approaching a woman, don't worry about it. Have some confidence. Who cares if she may not like you, or doesn't find you attractive, or doesn't want to talk? She's not going to take your birthday away, or get you fired from your job, or steal your car, or kick your dog. If she doesn't want to talk to you, this doesn't mean you're a bad guy. So, don't worry about it. Maybe she's not a very nice girl. Maybe she's having a bad day or night. Maybe you caught her by surprise and she's nervous. An initial response from a woman is to put up a wall from their apprehension. But look, you're not trying to steal her wallet, you're trying to meet and chat to see if there's a chance of moving forward. That's called having good intentions. That's a shocker that a guy would have good intentions. So, don't be afraid. You're not doing anything wrong.

I'm not saying that you approach every woman in the place and start talking. Reserve the approach for when you see a woman to whom you're attracted and you want to know more. And if it doesn't work out, who cares. You say, "Nice meeting you," and you move on. Successful people have short-term negative memory.

Forget about it. It's not *you*. It's the law of human nature.

◦◦ GO TIME... ◦◦

Here is the best approach that I know. It's simple. You approach her with purpose. Don't try to casually bump into her. If you try to casually bump into her, it's no longer casual and it will show. You look her in the eye, you smile big, and you extend your hand to shake. You say, "Hello, I'm *Chris*. It's nice to meet you." Keep it simple. You're objective is to meet her, so go and meet her. Given the circles you travel and the network of people that you associate with, she'll introduce herself back. She's not rude. She's a professional. She has some class. She's at that place for the same reason you are – to meet people and be social. And if she is rude, or has no class to say hello back, or is just too cool, she's not worth your time anyway. Walk away. No hard feelings. Your time is valuable. Cut this off quick. Forget about it. Remember, the most successful people have short-term negative memory.

Once the initial introduction is done, she may leave you out to dry for a few awkward seconds. That's OK. Don't panic. She's only waiting to see what you're there for. It's you that approached her. So relax, stay calm, and start chatting. Ask her if she's having fun. Ask her if she's from around here. Ask what she does for work. Ask her if YOUR ass looks fat in YOUR jeans. She will laugh, trust me. Just make small talk.

There's always going to be an objection or two that you will have to overcome. Remember, she's supposed to do this. She's not going to be a pushover; she's going to make you work a little. You have the complete arsenal here. You're equipped with all types of recipes for all different occasions. You have it all covered.

In a social situation, how would you feel if someone attractive walked up to you and introduced themselves? You'd probably feel pretty good. This person may not be your new best friend, but you'd probably be happy that this person had the confidence to approach you. Well, here's a secret: the girl you want to talk to is probably more nervous than you, so be the person who puts her at ease.

∾ THE BEAUTIFUL ONES ∾

All too often, guys are intimidated by the very beautiful. A woman of such beauty sometimes raises self-doubt. This is natural. Remember, the very best looking women are people too. They may be standing there looking unapproachable, but you don't really know what she's thinking or feeling. She could be nervous. She could be shy. Maybe it's she that has self-doubt, wondering why someone will not come up and say hello.

Say hello. Smile. That's all it takes. Here's a scenario we all know. You turn to your buddy and say to him, "What the heck is that girl doing with that guy? He's playing WAY above the rim with her…" You know what, it was "that guy," average Joe of average means, who humbly approached her, said hello, and started to chat. He took a little initiative, had confidence, and said hello. Point being – she's a person just like you. Be nice. Be polite. Don't be Eddie Haskell, but be friendly. She will respond accordingly. And if not, well you know what I say to that: short-term negative memory and she's probably not worth your time anyway.

∽ THE BLUEPRINT ∽

Asking a woman out can be like going to the gym for the first time. It seems a little overwhelming. But, once the trainer teaches you about the equipment, how to use it, and what it's used for, you're all set. You work out with confidence because you now know what you're doing. You have a plan. This is just like asking a woman out. Once you have a plan, the blue print, you will approach her with confidence as well.

You do this by sticking to the *blueprint*.

1. **Greeting** – we've already discussed the greeting
2. **Qualify** – you need to find out why she's there; does she have a boyfriend, is she seeing anyone, ever been married, are you waiting for someone? Your objective is to find out if there's potential in you cooking for her on the first date. You're trying to find out more information. The more you know, the easier it will be for the next step.
3. **Pitch** – Your "pitch" is going to be asking her to allow you to cook for her. "Look, one of these days let's get together and let me cook for you. You had no idea I could cook, did you? Of course not, how could you?" (Use the all-purpose sincere smile). "Well, I'll show you first-hand and we'll have a blast, I promise."

4. **Close** – As things are progressing, by the end of the evening you want to have some definite plans. Contact info, the day or evening, the menu plans, everything wrapped up except the evening itself.

Like a pro athlete, you need to be able to adjust to second-by-second changes on the field of play. The girl to whom you're speaking may respond in various ways. You need to be ready.

✎ • SHE SAYS, "NO THANKS," AND TURNS AWAY. ✎

Smile and say, "No problem," and go find another girl to approach. Do not waste your time trying to figure out why she responded negatively. It's just the roll of the dice. Keep moving. (As an unintended side benefit, at the very least she'll be impressed by your self-confidence. She may even reconsider. But that's her problem, not yours.)

✎ • SHE REPLIES, "BUT I JUST MET YOU. DO YOU THINK THAT'S APPROPRIATE FOR A FIRST DATE?" ✎

This is a great response! She's interested! Don't panic. You can counter with, "Well, this is our first date, right?" (Smile). "Me cooking for you will be the second date."

She may agree with you. Call it a second date because you're showing her you're not afraid of commitment, even if you really are. You're already committing to see her again.

If you're still met with apprehension, suggest cooking lunch, or brunch, or some sort of afternoon get-together – maybe by the pool. A daytime or mid-afternoon meeting is much less stressful. It's harmless. It's during the day. Anyone would feel more comfortable meeting during the day. It also shows that you don't have to be at the bar a few drinks in to want to see her. It's as harmless as meeting for a cup of coffee.

∽• SHE MAY SAY, "YES, I WOULD LIKE THAT…" ∽

She's closed. Nice job. This is the time a professional athlete signs the big contract. They do what's called, "agree in principle." She has agreed in principle to go out with you. And like the professional athlete's agent does for him, it's now time to work out the details.

1. **Suggest a day**. "Let's do it Thursday evening. That sounds good, right?" If Thursday is no good for her, suggest another day. She will agree to the second option. She's already agreed to go out with you in principle.

2. **Get her contact info**. But try to avoid any embarrassing scenes like writing a number on a napkin or anything to draw uncomfortable attention. Carry your business card and write her number on it. (If you don't have a business card, have some made or do it yourself.)

3. **Talk about the menu**. Find out what she likes by making suggestions. "Do you like seafood? I make the best shrimp scampi from here to Atlanta…" "Oh, OK what about chicken? I make a sautéed chicken breast with roasted Portobello mushrooms to die for…"

4. **You're always making suggestions**. You're trying to cook something you like and something you're comfortable cooking. It's easier to cook something that you like. She may make suggestions to you, and you agree with every one of them. Tell her that sounds good, but also tell her how she really needs to try your famous Tuna Tartare with Niçoise Vinaigrette, or your lump crab cakes, or chicken with Madeira wine. Flex your culinary muscles. Keep coming with the suggestions. You will find something she likes.

5. **Be proactive**. Have some confidence. *Be polite*. Don't leave yourself out there to be reactive to what she says or does. You direct the traffic. Control the ebb and flow. Think of it like baseball. You're a short stop and a ground ball's hit to you. Don't stand there on your heels and let the ball come to you.

You take control and charge the ball. Pick that grounder off on the first hop. This is being proactive.

6. **Don't look nervous**. She's just a woman you met, not the president of the United States. And remember, she may be more nervous than you. Put her at ease.

7. **Leave her alone**. You have the date planned, contact info, menu, and day. Don't start texting her every five minutes. In fact, save the texts for when you're both more comfortable with each other. Call her in a few days. It's hard to interpret the tone of a text so keep the human contact by calling. It's classy and shows effort. My 14-year-old niece could text someone. Don't be my 14-year-old niece.

So stick to the blueprint. Stay with the plan, and keep your eye on the prize. Only a small percentage of men have the effortless ability to meet and talk to women. You can be one of them. Once you read the directions, the task seems easier. Read the directions. Know the game plan. You don't have to watch film and study the way football coaches do, but read it and learn it. It will pay off.

CHAPTER 3: THE ESSENTIAL CULINARY TOOLS

"You plan for having the right cutlery, utensil, strainer, sheet tray, or sauce pan to execute the first date dining experience. When you're at home and you're cooking pasta, you're going to need a strainer. So, have a strainer available to you. It will be nerve-wracking to be cooking for your date and suddenly discover you don't have a slotted spoon, or a wire whisk, or a stainless steel mixing bowl when you need it."

THERE'S AN IMPORTANT SAYING for any tradesman: "The right tool for the job." This is even more important for the novice bachelor chef. My premise of "keep it simple" is why I want to spell out each item. The right tool for the job will minimize any snags or speed bumps that could occur. Our goal is to look top-chef nasty without having the top-chef skill. Having the right tools will help you achieve that.

You plan for having the right cutlery, utensil, strainer, sheet tray, or sauce pan to execute the first date dining experience. When you're at home and you're cooking pasta, you're going to need a strainer. So, have a strainer available to you. It will be nerve-wracking to be cooking for your date and suddenly discover you don't have a slotted spoon, or a wire whisk, or a stainless steel mixing bowl when you need it.

There's going to be some essential tools you need, and some that make your life easier. If in the future you plan on throwing a few first-date fiestas, make the small investment into your social life and pick these items up. Chances are you're going to find that you like to cook. Once you see a few of these dishes go off without a hitch and see someone else enjoying your creations, you will be hooked like any other professional chef. The reward is not only the successful first date, but also the gratification of seeing someone happy with your creations. Whether for a first date or not, the ability to cook and the right tools to do it will save you tenfold down the road. Think of the savings of not having to order take out, or eating out every night. The investment you make in the right equipment will pay off in the future.

THE MUST-HAVE TOOLS

1. A quality set of kitchen knives

You can purchase a quality set from $50 all the way up to $300. The knife set should come with a butcher block holding station to rest on your counter top. This adds a great aesthetic to the kitchen.

- Chef's knife or French knife
- Carving knife
- Boning knife
- Paring knife
- Serrated edge or bread knife
- Kitchen shears (scissors)
- Sharpening steel

2. The basic kitchen utensils

These also can be purchased as a set. This is much more cost effective to buy them as a set versus buying them individually. Buy this set as a stainless steel set. Try to stay away from the plastic sets. Your cost range is going to be anywhere from $50 to $150.

- Tongs
- Large spoon
- Slotted spoon
- Large wooden spoon
- Wire whisk
- Small spatula
- Slotted "fish" spatula
- Small mallet
- Set of ladles

3. The small wares

These small wares are most likely going to have to be purchased individually. Go to a home kitchen outlet store and grab the nearest sales associate. Tell them what you're trying to accomplish. They will steer you through the whole process as opposed to wandering around the store with no idea what you're doing.

- Colander
- Box grater
- 3 cookie sheets, each 9"x12"
- Ceramic casserole dish 9"x11"

- Conical Strainer (China Cap), hand held strainer
- Zester
- Hand-held juicer
- Stainless steel mixing bowl set of 3
- Pastry brush
- Rolling pin
- Vegetable peeler
- Pepper mill
- Hand-held can opener
- Kitchen towels (for handling hot pots/pans. Don't use your grandmother's pot holders – look like a pro)
- Rubber spatulas
- 1-quart measure
- 1-cup measure
- Set of measuring spoons
- Internal temperature thermometer

4. Pots and pans

You're able to buy most of these as a set. It will be sold as a 5-piece, 7-piece, or 9-piece set. So you will have to purchase the other items individually. Some of these sets can get expensive. However, you can purchase a quality set for around $75 to $100.

- 2-quart sauce pot
- 4-quart sauce pot
- 6-quart sauce pot
- 7" non-stick omelet pan or egg pan
- 7" fry pan
- 9" fry pan
- 11" fry pan
- Roasting pan
- 11" shallow sauce pot / rondeau

There will always be some items that you need that will make life more convenient if you're cooking often. These are things that you wouldn't think of and probably wouldn't have in the bachelor kitchen.

It's good to have some containers around for leftovers or leftover preparation items. It's good to wrap everything and keep it covered. You need a cutting board. The butcher block is going to be your "stage." This is where most of the show's going to take place.

- Hard plastic or Lexan cutting board
- Butcher block cutting board
- 9" roll of plastic wrap
- Aluminum foil
- Plastic re-usable storage containers
- Blender (for the blender drinks by the pool, too – very important)
- A corkscrew, wine opener, wine key
- All-in-one spice rack
- Coffee grinder

5. Wine glasses

Buy yourself a set of four red burgundy wine glasses and a set of 4 chardonnay wine glasses. The difference is in the size of the goblet. The red wine glasses will be larger than the white wine glasses. Now there are many types and sizes of wine glasses for all of the different varietals. Don't worry about this. You're not trying to be a sommelier. Not many people outside of sommeliers and people in the business know. In fact probably 95% of the people in the business don't know either. However, women usually drink wine, and they will know the basic rule – red wine glasses are larger than white wine glasses. So impress her by having both.

6. Wine rack

Buy yourself a small wine rack. You can either get one that sits on the counter top, or one that maybe doubles as a butcher block. I think it's important to have a few bottles of wine on hand at all times. You should have a few bottles of white, and a few bottles of different reds. Be a wine drinker. Wine is good for the soul. Drinking wine is relaxing. As a man, chances are that you will be partial to the bigger bolder reds – the Cabernets, Chiantis, Zinfandels, red Bordeaux, red Burgundies, Côtes du Rhônes. But also have some reds that are *easier* like the Pinot Noirs, Merlots, maybe a late harvest Cab. The whites are typically where the lady is going to stay. So have a Chardonnay, Pinot Grigio, Sauvignon Blanc, and some sort of sweeter varietals like a Riesling or Muscat.

7. Plate ware

The plate ware you select is going to serve as the backdrop or canvas to your culinary masterpieces. Not only should you select a quality set of plates, but keep them within a few color selections. The vibrant colors of many foods get lost in the plate when you have brightly colored or multi-colored plate ware. If in doubt, choose white. It's classy; it makes your food the centerpiece. Black looks good too, but sometimes darker foods get lost. Stick to basic round plates. All of these different shaped plates make me think of ordering tuna tataki at the sushi place. It looks funny serving a roast filet mignon on a tuna tataki plate. Symmetry is important when presenting any dish. Different sized plates make it very hard to put together a symmetrically pleasing dish. Just get white, and stick to rounds.

8. Coffee

Get a coffee maker of good quality. If you really want to do it right, have the capability of offering an espresso or cappuccino. An espresso machine can be purchased for around $50 to $80. It's classy and looks fantastic in the kitchen.

CHAPTER 4: THE BACHELOR'S HOME KITCHEN ESSENTIAL FOOD ITEMS

"I'm going to give you the outline to manage the Bachelor Home Kitchen. You never know when you will have the pop-up home-cooked first date. So when this happens, you'll be ready."

HAVING THE RIGHT PRODUCTS ON HAND is as important as having the right tools. I want to outline some of the staple goods you will need to have at all times. I'll break it down into a few different categories. Some will be perishable items (things that can spoil); some will be canned goods, and some frozen goods. Most will be products you would never think to have.

First let's take a minute to appreciate what it takes to be a successful chef. As the chef not only do you need to know how to cook, you're also responsible for every item in the kitchen. For every field greens salad on the menu, you have to make sure there are tomatoes on hand, lettuce, cucumbers, products to make the dressing, olive oil, vinegar, mayonnaise, sour cream, blue cheese, bread for croutons, the right plate ware to serve it, right on down to the salt and pepper you need to season things – everything. And that's just for a field greens salad. You need the ability to plan and speculate. That's one of the trickiest parts to the restaurant business, perishable inventory. You have to have the products on hand and make sure you use them. Cross utilization, specials, and different applications for the same product are how you do that. Or else you're taking money and throwing it in the garbage, literally.

Let's compare it to a retail clothing store. They both take business savvy. Have you ever heard of a shirt going bad? It may go out of style, but you can always discount it, sale price it, and recoup your money. You can't recoup spoiled lettuce, or sell fish with a few days age on it. It's *bad*, period. It's a volatile business. You're at the mercy of so many uncontrollable variables. Not only do you have to cook, but you have to *manage* as well.

I'm going to give you the outline to manage the Bachelor Home Kitchen. You never know when you will have the pop-up home-cooked first date. So when this happens, you'll be ready.

First let's talk about the **pantry items**. I refer to pantry items as products you need in order to execute anything you're going to cook. And they're kept in the pantry. Here are the basics.

- Kosher salt (coarse grain salt, preferable for having more control of application as opposed to the small grains of iodized table salt)
- Whole white peppercorns
- Whole black peppercorns
- Olive pomace oil (the third press of the olive, used to cook, sauté, pan fry. Olive pomace is used to cook because after the third press of the olive, all of the sediment is now gone which raises the burning point.)
- Extra-virgin olive oil (used for flavor in vinaigrettes, sauces, dressings, etc. This is the first press of the olive. All of the sediment/flavor is extracted and retained resulting in the darker more rich color and full flavor.)
- Vegetable oil
- Non-stick vegetable spray
- Spice rack (bought as a set)
- Balsamic vinegar
- Chicken bouillon cubes (to take the place of chicken stock)
- Sesame oil

Essential food to keep in the pantry:

∽ CANNED GOODS ∽

- Corn
- White navy beans
- Black beans
- Peas
- Peeled whole tomatoes in water
- Roasted red peppers
- Artichoke bottoms

∿ FOODSTUFFS ∿

- Peanuts
- Walnuts
- Dijon Mustard
- Coarse grain Dijon mustard
- Soy sauce
- Sesame oil
- Rice
- Couscous
- Pastas – angel hair, spaghetti, linguine, penne, fettuccine

Here are the **refrigerated products**. I don't expect you to keep a full inventory of produce at all times. You won't use it. You can always stop on the way home from work and pick up exactly what you need. However, here are a few items you can keep in the fridge that will last a long time. They're also essential in most of our cooking.

- Chopped garlic
- Eggs
- Tomatoes
- Mixed field greens (sold assorted in a bag)
- Lemons
- Limes
- Grated Parmesan cheese
- Whole butter, unsalted
- Pepperoncinis
- Mayonnaise
- BBQ sauce
- Whole unsalted butter
- Capers

In the **freezer**, always have these few items on hand:

- Boneless chicken breasts (purchased individually quick frozen, or IQF)

- Loaf of good bread – French, Italian, something to go with your meal
- Quality ice cream (pop-up dessert)

You should also keep two bottles of **cooking wine** – one white, and one red. You will find that wine will make up the base of most of our sauces.

If you have these products on hand, you could put together a hell of a meal without doing any shopping. With only your staple goods, here's an example of a meal you could whip up in 20 minutes.

Crusty Italian bread with butter and olive oil
*
Field greens salad with tomatoes and balsamic vinaigrette
*
Breast of Chicken Picatta with lemon, capers, garlic, and butter sauce over angel hair pasta or with rice pilaf

Not a bad menu with products you have on hand at all times. Break out the bread from the freezer, along with the chicken breast. Whip up a quick vinaigrette, which we'll get to, throw together your Picatta sauce (get to that, too) and it's on.

Remember that a valuable skill in the kitchen is the ability to *improvise*. When necessary to get the job done, a professional chef needs to know how to make do. It's a thinking man's game. You just never know what's going to happen. There are many uncontrollable variables when cooking for two or 20 or 200 people a night. Something breaks, it's not clean, and another department is using it…that's when a chef earns his money. The chef needs to know how to make things happen under any circumstance. This comes from nothing but experience. After a pro has been in a few thousand different crisis situations, he or she learns how to foresee potential snags. The same goes for you. As you try different recipes and see how the process works, you'll gain confidence and you'll learn how to roll with the punches.

As long as you're prepared, it's easy. Now you're ready. I've outlined everything you need to prepare yourself for the perfect home-cooked first date. We've spoke about how to get the date, what tools to have, and what basic foods to have at all times. We now start with the recipes. It's time for the fun stuff.

CHAPTER 5: CASUAL FIRST-DATE DINNERS

"I can whip a little something together and we can watch a movie..." First date.

To GET STARTED, we'll tackle the casual *"I'll whip a little something together and we can watch a movie"* first date.

During the qualifying process, it's important to gauge her interests and likes. Is she:

- The high-maintenance type
- The low-key type
- The happy-to-be-asked-out type?

You don't want to find yourself putting her in an uncomfortable environment. If she's the laid-back easygoing type, you don't want to throw down with a three-course dining experience. Save this for a more fitting occasion. And vice-versa; if she's a high-maintenance, "it's all about me" type, you don't want to stick chips and salsa on the table and tell her to dig in.

We're going to warm up with the casual, informal evening of a DVD and some homemade treats. These dishes will consist mostly of chopping, slicing, and dicing. There are a few dishes we will have to put heat to, but they're basic oven instructions. This will give you practice and help you gain confidence in the kitchen.

Remember - we're not building an atom bomb or performing brain surgery. It's only food. Relax and have fun. Try to execute the recipes with accuracy. But if you add a little more this, or not enough of that, don't worry. It's not the end of the world. Most likely, based on the ingredients we stick with, the dinner you prepare for her will come out tasting great.

HOMEMADE PITA CHIPS WITH WHITE BEAN HUMMUS AND FRESH ROSEMARY

Pita chips

- 1 package pita bread
- ½ cup extra virgin olive oil
- Salt and pepper to taste

Instructions

1. Cut pita bread into quarters or into triangles
2. Place on cookie sheet; brush both sides with olive oil and season with salt and pepper.
3. Bake in a 350-degree oven for 10 minutes, turning pita chips over after 5 minutes.
4. Set aside to cool.

White bean hummus

- 1 12-oz can of white navy beans, drained and rinsed
- ½ cup extra virgin olive oil
- ½ tsp chopped garlic
- 1 TBS tahini paste (sesame seed paste)
- 2 TBS finely chopped rosemary
- Juice of 1 lemon
- Salt and pepper to taste

Instructions

1. Drain white beans in a colander and rinse with cold water. Drain well.
2. In a blender, add beans, garlic, tahini paste, rosemary, and lemon juice.
3. While blender is running, slowly add your olive oil until white beans puree to a thick consistency.
4. Salt and pepper to taste.

NOTES

_____

_____

_____

_____

_____

_____

_____

_____

_____

_____

_____

_____

_____

_____

_____

_____

_____

_____

_____

_____

BRUSCHETTA WITH PARMA HAM, MOZZARELLA, BASIL, AND DICED TOMATOES

o Pronounced *BREW-SHET-AH*

- 1 loaf ciabatta bread or crusty Italian bread sliced into ½ inch slices
- ½ cup extra virgin olive oil
- ¼ lb. thin-sliced Parma ham (from your grocer's deli), julienned into thin strips
- 8 oz fresh mozzarella sliced (not shredded, in your deli section)
- 1 bunch fresh basil chiffonade (purchased in produce section, $1.99/package)
- 4 Roma tomatoes diced ¼ inch
- Salt and pepper to taste

Instructions

1. Place slice bread on a cookie sheet, brush both sides with olive oil, and bake in a 300-degree oven for 8 to 10 minutes. Allow to cool.
2. Cover toasted bread with mozzarella and julienned ham and bake in 400-degree oven until cheese is melted, about 3 to 5 minutes.
3. Remove from oven, top with diced tomatoes and basil, salt and pepper to taste, and serve immediately.

NOTES

_____

_____

_____

_____

_____

_____

_____

_____

_____

_____

_____

_____

_____

_____

_____

_____

_____

_____

_____

_____

_____

FRESH TOMATO SALSA

- 4 each 5 x 6 tomatoes, diced ¼ inch
- ½ cup finely chopped Spanish onion (white onion)
- 1 green bell pepper, diced
- 1 fresh jalapeño pepper, diced and de-seeded
- ¼ cup fresh chopped cilantro (produce section, $1.99/pk)
- Juice of 2 limes
- ¼ cup water
- Salt and pepper to taste
- 1 TBS ground cumin

Instructions

1. De-seed jalapeño by cutting in half lengthwise, then cut each half lengthwise. Run your knife through membrane, removing seeds.
2. Combine all ingredients and mix well.
3. Salt and pepper to taste, and allow to set up in refrigerator for at least an hour before serving.

Great served with tortilla chips, crostini, or serve with grilled chicken or fish as a sauce or an accompaniment.

NOTES

_____

_____

_____

_____

_____

_____

_____

_____

_____

_____

_____

_____

_____

_____

_____

_____

_____

_____

_____

_____

_____

BAKED BRIE IN PUFF PASTRY WITH APPLES AND BERRIES

- 2 small wheels of Brie cheese, usually 3 to 4 oz each
- 1 cup all purpose flour
- 1 package puff pastry (freezer section of grocery store near prepared frozen desserts)
- 2 eggs beaten
- 1 Granny Smith apple, sliced
- 1 pint raspberries
- 1 pint blue berries

Instructions

1. Spread flour over a flat work surface.
2. Lay thawed sheet of puff pastry flat on work surface.
3. Roll puff pastry with a rolling pin to slightly stretch and flatten.
4. Cut rolled puff pastry into 2 equal pieces.
5. Place Brie wheel in middle of puff pastry, stretching the pastry over the top to totally cover.
6. Cut away access pastry, and flip over to show smooth side.
7. Brush with egg and bake in a pre heated 350-degree oven for 8 to 10 minutes, or until puff pastry is golden brown and slightly "puffed".
8. Place baked brie on a serving platter and serve with sliced apples, and berries.

Serve with a loaf of crusty French baguette or table water crackers. This is a crowd pleaser.

NOTES

_____

_____

_____

_____

_____

_____

_____

_____

_____

_____

_____

_____

_____

_____

_____

_____

_____

_____

_____

_____

_____

MARINATED CHICKEN SATAY WITH PEANUT DIPPING SAUCE

Chicken satay

- Three 4-oz boneless skinless chicken breasts
- 1 cup soy sauce
- ¼ cup vegetable oil
- Juice of 1 lime
- 1 TBS honey

Instructions

1. Combine vegetable oil, soy sauce, lime juice, and honey in a bowl and combine well.
2. Slice chicken breasts into long strips and marinate in soy mixture for ½ hour.
3. Place on greased/sprayed cookie sheet and bake in a 350-degree oven for 10 to 12 minutes until cooked.
4. Skewer each satay with a bamboo skewer for service.

Peanut dipping sauce

- 2 cups creamy peanut butter
- 1 cup coconut milk
- ½ cup soy sauce
- ¼ cup honey
- ¼ cup sesame oil
- ¼ cup chopped cilantro
- ¼ cup finely chopped scallions
- 2 cups unsalted peanuts

Instructions

1. Combine all ingredients except peanuts in blender and blend until smooth.
2. Crush peanuts and fold into mixture.
3. Allow to sit for 1 hour prior to serving.

Serve on a large serving dish with the peanut dipping sauce placed in the middle and the satays arranged around.

NOTES

ROASTED MARINATED PORTOBELLO MUSHROOMS

- 6 large Portobello mushrooms
- 2 ½ cups extra virgin olive oil
- 1 ½ cups balsamic vinegar
- ¼ cup chopped basil
- ¼ cup chopped thyme
- ¼ cup chopped oregano
- Salt and pepper to taste

Instructions

1. Clean the bottoms of the Portobello mushrooms by running a spoon through the bottom to remove the "gills."
2. Place Portobello mushrooms on sprayed/greased cookie sheet.
3. Combine all ingredients in a bowl, mix well, and pour over Portobello mushrooms.
4. Season mushrooms with salt and pepper.
5. Bake in a 350-degree oven for 6 to 8 minutes until mushrooms are tender.
6. Serve hot or cold.

This is a versatile dish. You can serve this hot, cold, by itself, with a salad, as a side dish. What works well for this occasion is a small bed of mixed field greens tossed in olive oil, balsamic, and a little grated Parmesan.

NOTES

_____

_____

_____

_____

_____

_____

_____

_____

_____

_____

_____

_____

_____

_____

_____

_____

_____

_____

_____

_____

_____

THREE-CHEESE QUESADILLAS

- 1 package 12-inch flour tortillas (you can substitute any flavor tortilla – spinach, tomato, etc.)
- 1 12 oz. package shredded cheddar
- 1 12 oz. package shredded Monterey jack cheese
- 1 12 oz. package shredded Provolone cheese
- 1 cup chopped scallions
- 1 ea diced red or green bell pepper, or both
- Salt and pepper to taste

Instructions

1. Lay tortilla flat on work surface.
2. Spread the 3 cheeses evenly out on one half of the tortilla, equal to about 1 cup.
3. Spread the diced peppers and scallions evenly over the cheese.
4. Fold tortilla over to create a half-moon shape.
5. Preheat non-stick sauté pan over low to medium heat for 30 seconds and add ½ cup olive pomace oil.
6. Brown quesadillas on both sides for 1 minute, being careful not to let the pan get too hot.
7. Place quesadillas on greased cookie sheet and bake in a 350-degree oven for 4 minutes to melt cheeses.
8. Let cool for 30 seconds.
9. Cut your quesadilla into 4 triangle shaped pieces and serve warm.

Everyone likes quesadillas. They're so easy to prepare and make so much more of a statement than the typical chips and dip. You can stuff them with anything – grilled chicken, shrimp, scallops, bacon, ground beef…use your imagination.

NOTES

_____

_____

_____

_____

_____

_____

_____

_____

_____

_____

_____

_____

_____

_____

_____

_____

_____

_____

_____

_____

_____

PROSCIUTTO-WRAPPED SHRIMP WITH INFUSED OLIVE OIL

o   Pronounced *PRO-SHEW-TOE*

- 16 ea large shrimp, peeled and de-veined (16/20 grade or larger)
- ¼ lb thinly sliced prosciutto ham
- 1 package of bamboo skewers

Infused olive oil

- 3 cups extra virgin olive oil
- 6 sprigs rosemary
- 6 sprigs fresh thyme
- 8 ea whole black peppercorns
- 4 ea dried juniper berries
- 2 ea bay leaves
- 1 clove garlic, smashed
- 1 tsp chopped parsley
- 1 tsp chopped oregano
- Zest of one lemon

Instructions – infused oil

1. Combine all ingredients in a glass carafe or "Evian" glass bottle.
2. Allow infusing for 24 to 48 hours prior to service.
3. Refrigerate after 48 hours.

Instructions – shrimp

1. Wrap each shrimp with a thin slice of prosciutto.
2. Place shrimp on a sprayed cookie sheet, lined up parallel to each other in groups of 4.
3. Pass a 12-inch bamboo skewer through the 4 shrimp to secure the prosciutto.
4. Salt and pepper your shrimp, and bake in a 350-degree oven for 8 to 10 minutes.
5. To serve, brush shrimp generously with the infused olive oil.

These shrimp are great on their own, or serve with risotto or rice pilaf as an entrée. They're also good over a mixed green salad. Again, use your imagination. Great with a crisp Italian White wine.

NOTES

_____

_____

_____

_____

_____

_____

_____

_____

_____

_____

_____

_____

_____

_____

_____

_____

_____

_____

_____

_____

_____

CHAPTER 6: TAKING YOUR GAME UP A LEVEL

"Come over and I'll throw down top-chef-style..."
First date.

Now that you have some kitchen confidence, you can take it up a notch to the arrogant yet confident, *"Come over and I'll throw down top-chef-style..."* first date.

This is the high-maintenance-but-well-worth-it first date.

You met a vicious girl. You breezed right through the pitch. Last night you had your "A" game working. The only thing – you were so much on fire that you got carried away with the menu suggestions. By the looks of this girl, she's well worth it. You want to put on a good first show. You started suggesting some of the big guns. That's OK, have no fear. We're going to go through some of the more formal dishes in this chapter and throw in a few starter courses as well.

This is the fun stuff. She gets to watch as you work. You're both drinking wine. (Don't get drunk while you're cooking. Don't screw this up.) She's giggling and flirting, you're slicing and dicing, you have some music on, the table's set, and candles are out… it's on. This chapter is going to put to action everything that I'm trying to convey – *How to look top-chef nasty without being a top chef.*

We will start with the first course items. I'm going to lay out some small-plate salads and starters that are incredibly easy. Add a little bread and infused olive oil to start, a salad, the entrée, and dessert, and you now have a four-course dining experience.

STARTERS

FIELD GREENS SALAD WITH ROMA TOMATOES, HOMEMADE CROUTONS, BALSAMIC AND BASIL VINAIGRETTE, AND GRATED PARMESAN

Salad

- 3 cups assorted field greens, lightly packed
- 2 ea Roma tomatoes, cut into 8 wedges
- ½ cup grated parmesan

Croutons

- 2 cups crusty Italian bread cut into 1/4 inch cubes
- ½ cup extra virgin olive oil
- 1 tsp of each dry thyme, basil, oregano
- Salt and pepper

Instructions – croutons

1. Cut bread into ¼ inch cubes with bread knife or serrated knife.
2. Combine olive oil, dry herbs, and salt and pepper in bowl and mix well.
3. Toss croutons with olive oil mixture and place on a sprayed cookie sheet.
4. Bake in 350-degree oven for 10 minutes, turning croutons over after 5 minutes.

Balsamic vinaigrette

- 1 cup extra virgin olive oil
- 1/3 cup balsamic vinegar
- 2 TBS chiffonade of fresh basil
- Juice of 1 lemon
- Salt and pepper to taste

Instructions

1. Combine all ingredients in a bowl and mix well.
2. Salt and pepper to taste.

To serve

1. Toss greens with croutons, ½ cup of vinaigrette, and place on serving plates, centering the greens.
2. Place 4 tomato wedges on each plate, and sprinkle with fresh grated Parmesan.

The simplicity of this salad is its best quality. Its rustic ingredients and instructions are offset by the refined, centered presentation.

NOTES

_____

_____

_____

_____

_____

_____

_____

_____

_____

_____

_____

_____

_____

_____

_____

_____

_____

_____

_____

_____

_____

SPINACH SALAD WITH CRUMBLED FETA, ROASTED WALNUTS, OREGANO VINAIGRETTE

Salad

- 3 cups lightly packed fresh baby spinach leaves
- ½ cup cherry tomatoes, cut in half
- ¼ cup thinly sliced red onion
- ¼ cup olive pomace oil
- 1 cup walnut halves
- ½ cup crumbled feta cheese

Oregano vinaigrette

- 1 ¼ cup extra virgin olive oil
- 1/3 cup cider vinegar
- Juice of 1 lemon
- 3 TBS fresh chopped oregano
- ½ tsp sugar
- Salt and pepper to taste

Instructions – vinaigrette

1. Combine all ingredients and mix well. Set aside for service.

Instruction - walnuts

1. Toss walnuts with olive pomace oil.
2. Lay walnuts flat on sprayed cookie sheet and bake in a 350-degree oven for 4 to 6 minutes until lightly browned.
3. Allow to cool.

To serve

1. In a mixing bowl, add spinach, walnuts, tomatoes, and toss with vinaigrette.
2. Place spinach on serving plate and top with feta and shaved red onion.
3. Serve immediately.

NOTES

ICEBERG WEDGE SALAD WITH PUMPERNICKEL CROUTONS AND GORGONZOLA DRESSING

Salad

- 1 head of iceberg lettuce, cut into 8 equal wedges
- 1 ea 5 x 6 tomato, cut into 8 wedges
- ¼ cup shaved red onion

Pumpernickel croutons

- 2 cups ½ inch cubed pumpernickel or any black bread
- ½ cup extra virgin olive oil
- Salt and pepper to taste

Gorgonzola dressing

- 1 cup sour cream
- 1 cup mayonnaise
- ¼ cup heavy cream
- 1 cup crumbled Gorgonzola cheese (Italian blue cheese)
- 1 tsp of Worcestershire sauce
- Salt and pepper to taste

Instructions – croutons

1. Slice bread into ½ inch cubes with bread knife and place in large bowl.
2. Add olive oil and salt and pepper and toss well.

3. Lay croutons flat on cookie sheet and bake in a 350-degree oven for 8 to 10 minutes until croutons are crisp. Set aside to cool.

Instructions – dressing

1. Add sour cream, mayonnaise, cream, Worcestershire sauce to a large mixing bowl and mix well.
2. With rubber spatula, fold Gorgonzola cheese into dressing to mix well.
3. Salt and pepper to taste.
4. Allow to set up for 1 hour prior to service.
5. Best if made a day before.

To serve

1. Place a wedge of iceberg lettuce in the middle of plate.
2. Add 2 tomato wedges.
3. With a spoon, drizzle Gorgonzola dressing over the top of wedge.
4. Place red onion on top and sprinkle with pumpernickel croutons.

If your iceberg wedge appears to be too large a large portion, cut in half one more time. This hearty salad goes well with grilled steaks and chicken.

NOTES

_____

_____

_____

_____

_____

_____

_____

_____

_____

_____

_____

_____

_____

_____

_____

_____

_____

_____

_____

_____

EASY TOMATO BISQUE WITH ROSEMARY

- ¼ cup olive pomace oil
- 8 ea Roma tomatoes, roughly chopped
- 2 large chopped shallots (resembles a mini onion)
- 2 TBS chopped garlic
- 1 cup chicken stock (made from our chicken bouillon, see chapter 4)
- 2 ½ cups heavy cream
- 1 ea bay leaf
- 3 TBS of fresh finely chopped rosemary
- Salt and pepper to taste

Instructions

1. Preheat large saucepan over medium heat for 1 minute.
2. Add olive oil and sauté your shallot, garlic stirring constantly for about 1 minute.
3. Add tomatoes and allow cooking for 2 minutes.
4. Add chicken stock, cream, bay leaf and simmer over low heat for 10 minutes.
5. Add rosemary, and salt and pepper and simmer an additional 5 minutes.
6. Pull from heat and cool. Once cooled, blend in blender until smooth.
7. Reheat soup and salt and pepper to taste.

   - Note – If soup is still hot, blend in small amounts, 1/3 of the blender capacity at a time. The heat can cause the liquid to burst out of the top. Be very careful of this.

You can substitute any fresh herb you like – basil, thyme, sage…this is a versatile dish. Garnish with homemade croutons and fresh grated Parmesan cheese.

NOTES

_____

_____

_____

_____

_____

_____

_____

_____

_____

_____

_____

_____

_____

_____

_____

_____

_____

_____

_____

_____

_____

_____

CLASSIC SHRIMP COCKTAIL

- 1 lb or 16 large shrimp, shells on
- 3 quarts water
- 1 carrot, rough chopped
- 2 stalks celery, chopped
- 1 Spanish onion, chopped
- 3 lemons cut in half
- 5 ea bay leaves
- 2 cups pickling spice

Instructions

1. In a large stock pot, add 3 quarts water, carrot, celery, onion, lemon halves, bay leaves, and pickling spice and bring to a boil.
2. Add shrimp and cook for 5 minutes until shrimp turns reddish in color.
3. Strain shrimp well and cool in an ice water bath.
4. Remove the shell and legs and de-vein by running a knife down the back and removing the veins.
5. Wash shrimp well and refrigerate.

Cocktail sauce

- 1 cup chili sauce
- ½ cup ketchup
- 1/3 cup horseradish
- Juice of 1 lemon
- Dash Worcestershire sauce
- Salt and pepper to taste

Instructions

1. Add all ingredients together in a large mixing bowl and mix well.

NOTES

_____

_____

_____

_____

_____

_____

_____

_____

_____

_____

_____

_____

_____

_____

_____

_____

_____

_____

_____

_____

_____

_____

LUMP CRAB CAKE WITH SWEET GRAIN MUSTARD SAUCE

Crab cakes

- 1 can (16 oz) lump crab meat
- ¼ cup finely chopped chives
- ¼ cup + 1 TBS panko bread crumbs (Japanese-style coarse bread crumbs)
- 1 egg
- ¼ cup mayonnaise
- 1 tsp Dijon mustard
- Juice of 1 lemon
- Salt and pepper to taste

Instructions

1. Add mayonnaise, egg, Dijon, lemon juice to a large mixing bowl and mix well.
2. Add crabmeat, chives, breadcrumbs, and salt and pepper and fold into mix to combine well.
3. Form into crab cakes about 2 inches in diameter.

   - Note – If crab mixture appears to be too wet, add breadcrumbs 1 TBS at a time to bind.

Sweet grain mustard sauce

- 1 cup plain yogurt
- ½ cup coarse grain Dijon mustard
- 1 TBS Dijon mustard

- ½ cup honey
- Juice of 1 lime

Instructions

1. Combine all ingredients to large mixing bowl and mix well.

To serve

1. Preheat large sauté pan over medium heat.
2. Coat each crab cake with panko breadcrumbs and sauté in pan for 30 seconds per side until golden brown.
3. Remove cakes from pan and place on cookie sheet and bake in a 350-degree oven for 3 to 5 minutes to finish.
4. On a plate, add 2 oz of grain mustard sauce in the middle and place 2 crab cakes in the middle.
5. Serve while still hot.

NOTES

_____

_____

_____

_____

_____

_____

_____

_____

_____

_____

_____

_____

_____

_____

_____

_____

_____

_____

_____

_____

_____

_____

YELLOW FIN TUNA TARTARE WITH NIÇOISE VINAIGRETTE

o   Pronounced *NEE-SWAHZ*

•   6 oz fresh Yellow fin tuna, diced small, 1/8 inch dice

Vinaigrette

•   1 ½ cup extra virgin olive oil
•   ¼ cup white wine vinegar
•   2 tsp capers
•   ¼ cup sliced small   or chopped *haricots vert* (baby French green beans)
•   1 tsp finely minced red onion
•   1 TBS chopped parsley
•   1 TBS chopped fresh thyme
•   ½ TBS fresh lemon juice
•   Salt and pepper to taste

Instructions – vinaigrette

1.   Combine all ingredients in a large mixing bowl and mix well.

To serve

1.   Add small diced tuna to a large mixing bowl.
2.   Add vinaigrette to tuna (enough to incorporate well, ½ cup) and mix well to incorporate all ingredients.
3.   Place a 2 TBS portion of tuna mixture to the center of the plate.
4.   Drizzle remaining vinaigrette around the edge of the plate.

5. Serve with crusty bread, lavashe crackers, or table water crackers to give the dish texture.
6. Garnish with a fresh herb sprig, thyme, parsley, or chives.

- *Niçiose* refers to the classic salad preparation originated in the Cote d'Azur region of France, and the city of Nice. In lieu of the classic anchovies, olive, boiled egg, I like to use capers to give that acidy component, going a little better with the dish. However, recipes are subjective, and only a guideline. Please feel free to add finely chopped anchovies, or hardboiled egg as a garnish. It's also great served over crispy flatbread to give the dish texture.

NOTES

_____

_____

_____

_____

_____

_____

_____

_____

_____

_____

_____

_____

_____

_____

_____

_____

_____

_____

_____

_____

MAIN COURSES

SHRIMP SCAMPI WITH TOMATOES AND FRESH HERBS

- 12 large shrimp, peeled and de veined
- ¼ cup olive pomace oil
- ½ cup diced Roma tomatoes
- 1 TBS chopped garlic
- 1 cup white wine
- 4 oz or 1 stick unsalted whole butter
- Juice of 1 lemon
- 1 tsp chopped parsley
- 1 tsp chopped thyme
- Salt and pepper to taste

Instructions

1. Heat large sauté pan over medium heat for 30 seconds.
2. Add shrimp and cook for 1 minute.
3. Turn shrimp and add garlic and tomatoes and cook for another 30 seconds.
4. Add wine and simmer for 2 minutes until wine reduces by half.
5. Add butter and lemon juice and stir to incorporate butter.
6. Add lemon juice, herbs, and season with salt and pepper to taste.

NOTES

_____

_____

_____

_____

_____

_____

_____

_____

_____

_____

_____

_____

_____

_____

_____

_____

_____

_____

_____

_____

_____

_____

_____

ATLANTIC SALMON WITH CORN AND TOMATO FONDUE

- 2 ea 6 oz salmon filets
- ¼ cup olive pomace oil
- Salt and pepper

Corn and tomato fondue

- ½ cup olive pomace oil
- 3 ea Roma tomatoes, diced
- ½ cup julienne sun-dried tomatoes
- 8 oz can of corn, drained well
- ½ cup cherry tomatoes
- ¼ cup roughly chopped shallots
- ¼ cup chopped garlic
- ½ cup white wine
- 1 bay leaf
- ½ stick or 2 oz whole butter
- 1 TBS chopped thyme
- 1 TBS chopped oregano
- 1 TBS chopped rosemary
- Salt and pepper to taste

Instructions

1. Preheat large saucepan over medium heat for 1 minute.
2. Add shallots, garlic, sundried tomatoes and sauté for 30 seconds.
3. Add Roma tomatoes, cherry tomatoes, and corn and cook for 2 minutes.

4. Add wine and bay leaf, turn heat to low, and simmer for 4 minutes.
5. Add herbs and butter and stir to incorporate butter.
6. Salt and pepper to taste.

To serve

1. Pre heat large sauté pan over medium heat
2. Add olive oil, and cook salmon flesh side down for 1 minute.
3. Turn salmon over and cook for an additional 1 minute.
4. Remove salmon from pan and bake on cookie sheet in a 350-degree oven for 7 minutes until done.
5. Ladle 2 to 3 oz. fondue down onto the plate and serve salmon over the top.

   • Note – Salmon can also be grilled for a great smoked flavor to compliment fondue

NOTES

_____

_____

_____

_____

_____

_____

_____

_____

_____

_____

_____

_____

_____

_____

_____

_____

_____

_____

_____

_____

_____

_____

SAUTÉED SNAPPER FILET WITH LEMON BUTTER AND BASIL PAN SAUCE

- 2 ea 6 oz red or yellowtail snapper filets, skin off and de-boned (ask fish market to do this for you)
- ½ cup all-purpose flour
- 1/2 cup olive pomace oil
- Salt and pepper to taste
- 1 tsp chopped shallots
- 1 tsp chopped garlic
- 1 cup white wine
- Juice of 1 lemon
- ½ stick or 2 TBS whole butter unsalted
- ½ cup basil chiffonade, pronounced (*SHIFF-OH-NAHD*)
- Salt and pepper to taste

Instructions

1. Heat large sauté pan over medium heat for 1 minute.
2. Lightly coat both sides of snapper with flour and season with salt and pepper.
3. Add olive oil to pan and let heat for 15 seconds.
4. Sauté snapper flesh side down for 2 minutes and turn over.
5. Reduce heat to medium low and add shallots, garlic and cook for 20 seconds.
6. Remove snapper from pan, and bake in 350 – degree oven for 4 minutes until done.
7. Add wine and simmer on low for 2 minutes
8. Add lemon juice and swirl in butter to incorporate.
9. Finish with basil chiffonade and season with salt and pepper.

To serve – Place snapper on plate and pour sauce over the top.

NOTES

_____

_____

_____

_____

_____

_____

_____

_____

_____

_____

_____

_____

_____

_____

_____

_____

_____

_____

_____

_____

SEARED RARE TUNA WITH NAPA CABBAGE AND VEGETABLE QUICK FRY, SOY AND HONEY GLAZE

- 2 ea 6 oz yellow fin tuna steaks (ask the counter person to do this for you)
- ½ cup olive pomace oil
- Salt and pepper to taste
- ½ head Napa cabbage cut into thin shreds
- 1 ea julienne red bell pepper
- 1 ea julienne green bell pepper
- ½ red onion, julienned thin
- 1 TBS chopped garlic
- 1 tsp minced fresh ginger
- ¼ cup white wine
- ½ cup soy sauce
- 1 TBS honey
- 1 TBS butter
- Salt and pepper to taste

Instructions

1. Heat large sauté pan over medium heat for 1 minute.
2. Salt and pepper tuna steaks, add olive oil to pan and sear tuna for 1 minute on each side.
3. Remove tuna from pan and set aside.
4. Add garlic, ginger, and red onion and sauté for 30 seconds.
5. Add peppers and Napa cabbage and sauté for another 1 minute.

6. Add wine, soy, and let simmer for 30 seconds.
7. Finish with honey and butter and mix well in pan to incorporate.

To serve

1. Add large spoonful of rice to center of the plate and form into ring.
2. Place stir-fry vegetables in center, and top with rare tuna.
3. Serve immediately.
4. Note – This dish is typically served rare or medium rare. To cook tuna more, place tuna on greased cookie sheet and bake for an additional 2 to 3 minutes.

NOTES

_____

_____

_____

_____

_____

_____

_____

_____

_____

_____

_____

_____

_____

_____

_____

_____

_____

_____

_____

_____

_____

_____

TOURNEDOS OF BEEF TENDERLOIN WITH RATATOUILLE AND WILD MUSHROOMS

o   Pronounced *TOR-NAH-DOSE*
o   Pronounced *RAT-TAT-TOO-EE*

- 4 ea, 3 oz beef tenderloin medallions
- ¼ cup olive pomace oil
- ½ cup sliced shiitake mushrooms
- ½ cup sliced button mushrooms
- 1 tsp chopped garlic
- 1 tsp chopped shallots
- ¼ cup white wine
- 1 TBS chopped fresh rosemary
- 2 TBS whole butter
- Salt and pepper to taste

Ratatouille

- ½ cup olive pomace oil
- ½ cup diced zucchini, ¼ inch dice
- ½ cup diced yellow squash, ¼ inch dice
- ¼ cup diced green bell pepper, 1/8 inch dice
- ¾ cup diced Roma tomatoes, ¼ inch dice
- 1 tsp chopped garlic
- 1 tsp chopped shallot
- 1 tsp chopped thyme
- 1 tsp chopped oregano
- 1 tsp whole butter

Instructions – Ratatouille

1. Pre heat large saucepan over medium heat for 1 minute.
2. Add olive oil and add garlic, shallot, and green pepper and sauté for 30 seconds.
3. Add zucchini, yellow squash and sauté for another 2 minutes.
4. Reduce heat to medium low and add tomatoes, cooking for another 2 minutes.
5. Finish with thyme, oregano, and stir in butter to incorporate.
6. Salt and pepper to taste.

Instructions – tournedos

1. Preheat large sauté pan over medium/high heat for 1 minute.
2. Add olive oil and let heat for 30 seconds.
3. Place tournedos in pan and sear for 2 minutes to brown.
4. Turn steaks over, reduce heat to medium and add garlic, shallots, and mushrooms.
5. Let tournedos cook for another 3 minutes and pull from pan and set aside.
6. To mushrooms, add wine and let simmer for 30 seconds.
7. Finish with rosemary and butter mixing well to incorporate.
8. Salt and pepper to taste.

To serve

1. Spoon Ratatouille into center of the plate.
2. Place beef tournedos over the top, and finish with sautéed mushrooms over the beef.

NOTES

_____

_____

_____

_____

_____

_____

_____

_____

_____

_____

_____

_____

_____

_____

_____

_____

_____

_____

_____

BREAST OF CHICKEN WITH ROASTED PORTOBELLO MUSHROOMS AND MADEIRA WINE BUTTER SAUCE

- 4 ea 6 oz boneless skinless chicken breasts
- ½ cup olive pomace oil
- ½ cup all purpose flour
- 2 tsp chopped shallots
- 1 tsp chopped garlic
- 1 ½ cups Madeira wine
- 1 ea bay leaf
- 1 stick whole butter
- Salt and pepper to taste

Roasted Portobello mushrooms

- 4 large Portobello mushrooms
- 2 cups extra virgin olive oil
- ¾ cup balsamic vinegar
- 1 TBS thyme
- 1 TBS oregano
- Salt and pepper to taste

Instructions – Portobello mushrooms

1. Clean mushrooms by trimming off the bottoms with a knife.
2. Combine olive oil, balsamic, herbs in a bowl.
3. Place mushrooms flat on cookie sheet and pour olive oil mixture over the top of each mushroom.
4. Bake in a 350-degree oven for 8 minutes until mushrooms are tender.

Instructions – chicken

1. Pre heat large sauté pan over medium heat for 1 minute.
2. Dredge or lightly coat chicken breast with flour.
3. Add olive oil to pan and sauté chicken on one side for 2 minutes.
4. Turn chicken over and continue to cook for 1 minute.
5. Add shallots and garlic and sauté for 30 seconds.
6. Pull pan from heat, add Madeira wine, and return pan to heat.
7. Pull chicken from pan and bake in 350-degree oven for an additional 5 minutes.
8. Add butter and bay leaf to pan and swirl butter into sauce.
9. Remove bay leaf prior to service.

To serve

1. Place 2 roasted Portobello mushrooms onto the center of the plate.
2. Place 2 chicken breasts over the top and pour Madeira sauce over the chicken to finish.
3. Note – this may be a large portion for one person, so do not hesitate to serve only one chicken breast.

NOTES

_____

_____

_____

_____

_____

_____

_____

_____

_____

_____

_____

_____

_____

_____

_____

_____

_____

_____

_____

_____

_____

_____

VEAL PICATTA WITH WINE, CAPERS, GARLIC, AND BUTTER SAUCE

- 4 ea 3 oz veal loin medallions (*ask butcher for availability, if not use veal top round medallions. Ask butcher to tenderize*)
- ½ cup olive pomace oil
- ¼ cup flour
- Salt and pepper
- 1 cup white wine
- ¼ cup capers
- 1 tsp chopped garlic
- Juice of 1 lemon
- ¼ lb whole butter
- 1 TBS basil chiffonade

Instructions

1. Dredge veal medallions with flour and season with salt and pepper.
2. Preheat large sauté pan for 1 minute.
3. Sauté veal medallions on 1 side for 1 minute.
4. Turn veal over and add capers, garlic and cook for 1 minute being careful not to burn.
5. Add wine, let simmer for 30 seconds, and remove veal and set aside.
6. Simmer wine for 1 minute and add lemon juice, butter, and swirl to make sauce.
7. Finish with salt and pepper and basil chiffonade.

NOTES

_____

_____

_____

_____

_____

_____

_____

_____

_____

_____

_____

_____

_____

_____

_____

_____

_____

_____

_____

_____

_____

EASY SIDE DISHES

These side dishes are all basic and all interchangeable. Add one of these side dishes to one of your entrees to complete your dish.

The beauty is you're free to use your imagination and add what you like. If you want to make the couscous "herbed couscous," then add chopped fresh herbs. If you want to make tomato and basil rice pilaf, add diced tomatoes and basil to the rice. They sound fantastic, and are also so very simple. Cooking is easy. Once you have a few basics, you can begin to branch off and be creative.

BASIC COUSCOUS

o   Pronounced *COOS-COOS*

- 1 cup couscous, medium grain *(be careful not to buy Israeli couscous, for the kernels are much larger and not meant for this recipe)*
- 2 ¼ cups chicken stock or broth
- 1 ea bay leaf
- 1 TBS chopped fresh thyme
- 1 TBS chopped parsley
- 1 TBS whole butter
- Salt and pepper to taste

Instructions

1. Heat chicken broth and bay leaf in saucepan to a boil.
2. Pour dry couscous into a separate large mixing bowl.
3. When chicken broth comes to a boil, pour over the top of couscous and mix well.
4. Cover bowl with plastic wrap and set aside to allow cooking for 10 minutes.
5. Remove plastic wrap and fold in parsley, thyme, butter, and salt and pepper.
6. Mix well with a fork to fluff couscous, in other words to separate the kernels to give a fluffy and light texture.

Add whatever you like to couscous – tomatoes, basil, diced vegetables, herbs, nuts, etc. This is a versatile side dish that can go with anything. Couscous is a great alternative for something different as a side dish.

NOTES

BASIC RICE PILAF

- 2 cups rice
- ½ cup diced onion, ¼ inch dice
- 1 TBS chopped garlic
- 2 TBS butter
- 4 cups chicken stock or broth
- 2 ea bay leaf
- Salt and pepper to taste

Instructions

1. Heat saucepan over medium heat for 1 minute.
2. Add butter, onion, and garlic and sauté for 1 minute.
3. Add rice and stir constantly for 30 seconds to coat each kernel with butter.
4. Add chicken broth, bay leaf, and bring to boil.
5. Once boiling, reduce heat to medium low and simmer until rice absorbs all the liquid.
6. Once all liquid is absorbed, pull from heat, let sit for 5 minutes, and season with salt and pepper.
7. Fluff rice with a fork to separate all kernels.

NOTES

_____

_____

_____

_____

_____

_____

_____

_____

_____

_____

_____

_____

_____

_____

_____

_____

_____

_____

_____

_____

_____

_____

ROASTED NEW POTATOES

- 3 cups red or new potatoes, cut in half or quartered if large
- 2 cups extra virgin olive oil
- 2 TBS chopped garlic
- 2 TBS chopped fresh rosemary
- 1 TBS chopped parsley
- Salt and pepper to taste

Instructions

1. Combine olive oil with garlic, herbs, and salt and pepper.
2. Toss potatoes with olive oil mixture and place potatoes on cookie sheet.
3. Bake in a 350-degree oven for 12 to 15 minutes until potatoes are fork tender.

NOTES

_____

_____

_____

_____

_____

_____

_____

_____

_____

_____

_____

_____

_____

_____

_____

_____

_____

_____

_____

_____

_____

BASIC RISOTTO RECIPE

- ½ lb whole butter
- ½ cup diced onion
- 1 TBS chopped garlic
- 2 cups Arborio rice (a shorter, thicker grain of Italian rice)
- 4 cups chicken stock
- ¼ cup grated Parmesan cheese
- Salt and pepper to taste

Instructions

1. Bring chicken broth to a boil, and then turn heat down to a simmer.
2. In a separate saucepan, pre heat this pan over medium heat for 1 minute.
3. In the separate saucepan, add ½ of the butter, onion, and garlic and sauté for 30 seconds.
4. Add Arborio rice and stir constantly to coat each kernel with butter.
5. Slowly add hot chicken stock 6 to 8 oz at a time, continuously stirring.
6. As rice absorbs liquid, constantly stir the rice.
7. When liquid is absorbed, pull from heat and mix in the remaining butter, Parmesan, and season with salt and pepper.

Feel free to add whatever herbs or flavoring you like.

NOTES

_____

_____

_____

_____

_____

_____

_____

_____

_____

_____

_____

_____

_____

_____

_____

_____

_____

_____

_____

_____

_____

_____

CHAPTER 7: GRILLING OUTSIDE

"Let's spend the afternoon by the pool. I'll fire up
the grill and make some blender drinks..."
First date.

LET'S STEP OUTSIDE into the relaxing environment of the *"Let's spend the afternoon by the pool. I'll fire up the grill and make some blender drinks"* first date.

Here in Florida, every day's a great day to eat *al fresco*. The sun's always shining, the weather's warm, and the grill's fired up. Who's not in a good mood at a cookout? Like most of us who live here, a cookout reminds us of easy summer days. Living in the four seasons makes you cherish each summer day.

Wherever you live, from Maine to Hawaii, you can get the feeling of summer by firing up the grill and getting out the blender. The sound of the blender is the perfect backdrop for your any-season cookout. Frozen drinks are fun, easy to drink, and a great way to take the heat off of the first date – literally. It's relaxing. The mid-afternoon warmth is tranquil.

Let's tell it like it is here, too. When you want to check out a girl's appearance, there are two places that tell all – the beach and the gym. In a dark nightclub, artfully chosen clothing and labor-intensive makeup can make a woman appear to be someone she's not. But at the beach in a bikini, there's no hiding.

But let's get back to business. The best thing about this *al fresco* date is the spread you're going to prepare. A few different cold salads, maybe some grilled marinated vegetables, and steaks and chops that will draw the neighbor's attention as they hit the grill. Grilling is a great way to eat. It's health-conscious, mess-free, and oh-so-good.

Chapter 7 is one of my favorite first-date scenarios. The lack of pretense, the food, the blender drinks – all the pressures are gone. Even if things aren't clicking, you're still going to have a good time. At a worst case, you can turn the flat screen around and watch the game through the window. Although with this setup, things will be clicking on all eight cylinders. But as casual a setting as it may be, it still takes thought and a little work.

She'll recognize the effort. By throwing this scenario together, you're bound to impress.

MARINATED TOMATO AND CUCUMBER SALAD

- 3 ea 5x6 tomatoes, cut in half and then sliced thin
- 2 ea cucumbers, peeled, seeded, and sliced thin
- ½ cup thinly sliced red onion
- ½ cup sliced Kalamata olives
- 1 ½ cups extra virgin olive oil
- ½ cup balsamic vinegar
- Juice of 1 lemon
- ¼ tsp chopped garlic
- 1 TBS chopped thyme
- 1 TBS chopped oregano
- 1 TBS chopped parsley
- Salt and pepper to taste
- ¾ cup grated Parmesan cheese

Instructions

1. De-seed your cucumber by splitting in half lengthwise and then running a spoon down the middle to remove the seeds.
2. Combine sliced tomatoes, cucumbers, onion, and olives in a large mixing bowl.
3. In separate mixing bowl, combine the rest of the ingredients and mix well.
4. Pour olive oil mixture over the tomatoes/cucumber and toss well.
5. Allow the salad to marinate for ½ hour to 2 hours prior to serving, or this salad can be made 1 day in advance.

NOTES

_____

_____

_____

_____

_____

_____

_____

_____

_____

_____

_____

_____

_____

_____

_____

_____

_____

_____

_____

_____

_____

BLACK BEAN AND RICE SALAD WITH BELL PEPPERS AND LIME

- 1 ea 12 oz can of black beans, rinsed thoroughly
- 1 cup cooked rice
- ½ cup diced green pepper
- ½ cup diced red pepper
- ½ cup diced yellow pepper
- 1 cup vegetable oil
- ½ cup rice vinegar
- Juice of 2 limes
- ½ cup chopped cilantro
- 2 TBS ground cumin
- 1 tsp ground coriander
- Salt and pepper to taste

Instructions

1. Combine black beans, rice, and diced peppers in a large mixing bowl and toss well.
2. In a separate bowl, mix the remaining ingredients together.
3. Pour the dressing into the black beans and rice and toss well.
4. Salt and pepper to taste.
5. Allow salad to marinate for ½ hour to 2 hours prior to serving.

NOTES

_____

_____

_____

_____

_____

_____

_____

_____

_____

_____

_____

_____

_____

_____

_____

_____

_____

_____

_____

_____

_____

MEDITERRANEAN NEW POTATO SALAD

- 3 cups new potatoes, cooked, cooled, and quartered
- 1 cup julienned green bell pepper
- ½ cup diced celery
- ¼ cup finely diced red onion
- ½ cup capers
- 1 cup crumbled feta
- 1 cup extra virgin olive oil
- ¼ cup chopped fresh oregano
- ¼ cup chopped parsley
- Juice of 1 lemon
- Salt and pepper to taste

Instructions

1. Cut raw potatoes into quarters and boil for 15 minutes or until tender to the fork.
2. Strain well and cool in refrigerator.
3. Add cool potatoes to a large mixing bowl and add green pepper, celery, red onion, capers, and feta and toss well.
4. In a separate mixing bowl, add the rest of the ingredients and mix well.
5. Combine the dressing to the potatoes and toss well.
6. Allow to set up for ½ hour to 2 hours prior to service.

NOTES

_____

_____

_____

_____

_____

_____

_____

_____

_____

_____

_____

_____

_____

_____

_____

_____

_____

_____

_____

_____

_____

_____

CLASSIC MACARONI SALAD

- 3 cups cooked macaroni
- 1 ½ cups diced celery
- ½ cup diced red onion
- 2 ea chopped hardboiled egg
- 1 cup mayonnaise
- 1 TBS Dijon mustard
- 1 TBS celery seed
- Salt and pepper to taste

Instructions

1. Mix macaroni, celery, onion, and egg in a large mixing bowl.
2. In a separate mixing bowl, mix mayonnaise, mustard, celery seed together and add to macaroni.
3. Toss all ingredients well, salt and pepper to taste.
4. Note – the hardboiled egg is optional. If you don't like it, don't use it.

NOTES

_____

_____

_____

_____

_____

_____

_____

_____

_____

_____

_____

_____

_____

_____

_____

_____

_____

_____

_____

_____

_____

_____

IMPORTANT TIPS ON GRILLING

Here are some important tips when it comes to grilling. There's much more to it than lighting the grill, throwing a piece of meat on it, and cooking the piece until its "ready." There are basic techniques that once you understand why, and then practice, you will then be able to truly call yourself the grill master.

Salt and pepper

- ✓ Season everything. This is the number one rule in any cooking. The difference between a good cook and a great cook is salt and pepper. Especially when grilling.
- ✓ Aggressively season your meats/fish prior to grilling. A lot of your salt and pepper will be left on the grill.
- ✓ Re-season your meats/fish at least once while cooking. Something as simple as seasoning everything is the difference between a good steak and a great steak.

The importance of marinating

- ✓ Marinating is essential to imparting flavor. It also helps to tenderize. However, there are a few things you need to know when making your marinades.
- ✓ Contrary to the season-everything stuff, do not add salt to any of your marinades. Salt has the ability to "cure" your product. Curing is a way of preserving foods. It makes the foods bacteria-free and safe to eat. For instance, you have heard of salt-cured meats? The texture of something salt-cured is like beef jerky. Don't turn your steaks into beef jerky.
- ✓ If you plan on marinating anything for longer than 1 hour, stay away from acidic ingredients. This too will cure your food.

Citric acid (lemon/lime juice, orange juice), vinegar, and soy are all great ingredients for marinating, but be careful not to marinate too long. Use these products to marinate foods, but as an added ingredient to your olive oil or whatever you're using. Be careful not to marinate with acidic ingredients for longer than an hour.

✓ Foods that work great for marinating are aromatic herbs like rosemary, thyme, and oregano. Also, the zest of any citrus fruit works well. Zest is the very outer layer of skin of any citrus fruit. Zest is what's outside the pith, or bitter white membrane of any citrus. You don't want to use the pith. Bay leaf imparts a beautiful flavor on meats and fish. Garlic and shallot, onion all work well too. A little olive oil, fresh herbs, fresh cracked pepper, bay leaf, garlic and shallots make a hell of an all-purpose marinade; even perhaps add a little shake of Worcestershire sauce. Go heavy on the fresh herbs though, and you won't go wrong.

Hot side and carryover side of the grill

✓ When you light your grill, it's very important to have a hot side, and what I call the "carryover" side of the grill. The carryover side is going to be at a medium to low heat. The hot side is going to be for searing and marking your meats/fish, and the carryover side is going to be for continuing to cook without charring the outside. I always demand that grills have the hot side and carryover side in any kitchen I work in.

✓ The hot side is used to sear your foods. To sear your food means to first cook on an extremely hot surface to sear or lock in the flavors and juices. The best analogy I can think of is the idea of cauterizing something to seal it up. You sear meats and fish to lock up and seal in the essential flavors and juices.

✓ Once you sear your meats and fish on both sides, it's then time to move your product over to the carryover side of the grill. The idea behind this is to continue to cook your product without it becoming too charred or burnt on the outside. As all of you know I'm sure, if you try to cook a steak on the grill that's turned all the way to high, by the time it's medium rare, it's cooked like a piece of charcoal. The grill's too hot. That's why you first sear the meats/fish on the hot side. Once you've seared in the flavors, you then move it to the carryover side to continue to slowly and fully cook. This is the difference between throwing a piece of meat on the grill, and properly cooking a piece of meat or fish on the grill.

Grill marks or diamond marks

- ✓ Have you ever wondered how steaks at a restaurant get those beautiful diamond-pattern grill marks on them? There's a simple technique to achieving this. It's called the "2 o'clock to 5 o'clock" method.
- ✓ You achieve this by placing your steak on the hot side of the grill to resemble the 2 o'clock setting of a clock. You allow it to sear for about 45 seconds to 1 minute. You then rotate the steak to the 5 o'clock position and allow it to sear again.
- ✓ Note – whatever you grill, sauté, etc., always start with the "presentation" side first, or the side that will be presented upwards on the plate.
- ✓ The turning of the steak from 2 o'clock to 5 o'clock will create diamond marks. Repeat this for the other side of the steak as well. After this is done, it's now time to move your steak over to the carryover side.

Salt and pepper everything, marinate prior to cooking, the hot side/carryover side theory, and the method behind the proper grill marks. Whether you're grilling out for your first date or working in a five-star kitchen, these tips are the mainstay to properly grilling anything. Now you have the tools to truly call yourself the grill master.

GRILLED AND CHILLED MARINATED ASPARAGUS WITH GRATED PARMESAN

- 2 bunches asparagus, trimmed to 3 inch length
- ¾ cup grated Parmesan
- 2 cups olive pomace oil
- 1 cup balsamic vinegar
- 1 ea chopped shallot
- 1 TBS chopped garlic
- ¼ cup chopped fresh rosemary
- ¼ cup chopped thyme
- 1 ea bay leaf
- Salt and pepper to taste

Instructions

1. Trim the stem-side edges off of asparagus to make them about 3" long and lay flat on cookie sheet.
2. Combine olive oil, balsamic, shallot, garlic, fresh herbs, and bay leaf and pour half over asparagus. Allow marinating time of at least 15 minutes to ½ hour.
3. Grill asparagus over medium to low heat for 1 minute a side.
4. Return asparagus to cookie sheet and pour remaining marinade over cooked asparagus.
5. Cool in refrigerator to cool, serve with grated Parmesan over the top.

NOTES

GRILLED MARINATED PORTOBELLO MUSHROOMS

- 6 large Portobello mushrooms
- 3 cups olive pomace oil
- 1 cup balsamic vinegar
- ¼ bunch basil
- ¼ bunch thyme
- ¼ bunch oregano
- Salt and pepper to taste

Instructions

1. Trim off the bottoms of the Portobello mushrooms by scraping the bottoms with a spoon to remove the "gills."
2. Combine the rest of the ingredients in a bowl and pour over Portobello mushrooms after laying the mushrooms on a sprayed cookie sheet.
3. Grill on hot side for 1 minute per side.
4. Move Portobello mushrooms to the carryover side and allow to cook an additional 2 minutes until tender.
5. Serve hot or cold.

NOTES

_____

_____

_____

_____

_____

_____

_____

_____

_____

_____

_____

_____

_____

_____

_____

_____

_____

_____

_____

_____

_____

_____

JUMBO SHRIMP WITH ORANGE AND ROSEMARY GLAZE

- 16 ea large shrimp, peeled and de veined
- 1 cup olive pomace oil
- 1/3 cup orange juice, or juice of 3 oranges
- 1 TBS chopped fresh rosemary
- Salt and pepper to taste

Orange rosemary glaze

- 2 cups orange juice
- 2 TBS orange zest
- 1 TBS rice vinegar
- ½ cup honey
- ¼ cup chopped fresh rosemary
- 1 bay leaf
- Salt and pepper to taste

Instructions – shrimp

1. Combine olive oil, orange juice, and rosemary to create marinade.
2. Marinate shrimp for 15 minutes to a ½ hour.

Instructions – orange rosemary glaze

1. Zest the oranges by grating oranges on the fine side of box grater to remove only the zest. Be careful not to grate down into the pith – this is the bitter portion of the peel.
2. Combine all ingredients and mix well.

Cooking instructions

1. Heat glaze in a saucepan on a portion of the carry over side of grill.
2. Remove shrimp from marinade and gently pat off the excess marinade with a paper towel.
3. Grill shrimp on hot side for 1 minute per side.
4. Transfer shrimp to carry over side for an additional 2 minutes.
5. Brush generously with glaze prior to serving.

NOTES

NEW YORK STRIP STEAK WITH MAÎTRE D'HÔTEL BUTTER

- 2 ea New York strip steaks, 10 oz

Marinade

- 1 cup olive pomace oil
- 1 TBS chopped shallot
- 1 TBS chopped garlic
- 1 TBS chopped rosemary
- 1 TBS chopped thyme
- 1 TBS fresh cracked black pepper
- 2 ea bay leaf
- 1 TBS Worcestershire sauce

Maître d'hôtel butter

- ¼ lb or 1 stick whole butter softened to room temperature
- ½ tsp chopped garlic
- 2 TBS chopped parsley
- 1 tsp chopped fresh thyme
- Zest and juice of 1 lemon
- 1 tsp white wine
- 1 tsp Worcestershire sauce
- Salt and pepper to taste

Instructions – marinade

1. Mix all ingredients well.

Instructions – maître d'hôtel butter

1. Soften butter by leaving out at room temperature until soft enough to mix with stiff wire whisk.
2. Combine all ingredients in a large mixing bowl and mix well with large kitchen spoon or stiff wire whisk to incorporate all ingredients.
3. If you have a small kitchen aide mixer, place all ingredients in bowl and beat the butter for 2 minutes until light and airy.
4. Remove from bowl and place in a refrigerator safe container. Use immediately or you can keep in refrigerator up to 1 week.

Instructions – steaks

1. Pour half of the marinade onto a cookie sheet and spread out to cover bottom.
2. Marinate steaks by placing them in marinade on cookie sheet and pouring the remainder over the top. Allow steaks to marinate for at least ½ hour.
3. Cook steaks on hot side of grill for 4 minutes a side, turning to create "diamond marks."
4. Transfer to hot side and allow cooking an additional 3 to 4 minutes until desired degree of doneness.
5. Serve steaks while still hot with a generous spoonful of maître d'hôtel butter over the top and allow melting.

NOTES

_____

_____

_____

_____

_____

_____

_____

_____

_____

_____

_____

_____

_____

_____

_____

_____

_____

_____

_____

_____

_____

SWORDFISH STEAK WITH CITRUS BARBEQUE GLAZE

- 2 ea swordfish steaks, 6 oz
- ¼ cup olive pomace oil
- Salt and pepper to taste

Citrus barbeque glaze

- 2 cups barbeque sauce
- ¾ cup honey
- Juice and zest of 1 orange
- Juice and zest of 2 limes
- Juice and zest of 1 lemon
- 1 tsp chopped thyme
- 1 tsp chopped parsley
- 1 TBS whole butter

Instructions – barbeque glaze

1. Zest your citrus fruit by grating the skin with a box grater to get the zest.
2. Cut all citrus in half and squeeze juice into a medium saucepan, being careful not to get any seeds in the sauce pan.
3. Combine all ingredients into medium saucepan except for butter and simmer on low heat for 8 to 10 minutes.
4. Add butter and mix well once sauce is simmering.

Instructions – swordfish

1. Salt and pepper swordfish, brush with olive oil, and grill on hot side of the grill for 2 minutes a side, turning to create diamond marks.
2. Transfer to carry over side and cook for an additional 2 to 3 minutes.
3. Brush generously with barbeque glaze while on carry over side.
4. Prior to serving, brush one more time with warm barbeque sauce.

NOTES

_____

_____

_____

_____

_____

_____

_____

_____

_____

_____

_____

_____

_____

_____

_____

_____

_____

_____

_____

_____

_____

GRILLED BREAST OF CHICKEN WITH HERB-INFUSED OLIVE OIL

- 4 ea 4 oz boneless skinless chicken breasts
- ¼ cup olive pomace oil
- Salt and pepper to taste

Marinade

- 1 cup olive pomace oil
- 1 tsp chopped garlic
- 1 ea chopped shallot
- 1 TBS chopped thyme
- 1 TBS chopped rosemary
- 1 TBS Worcestershire sauce
- 1 TBS fresh cracked black pepper
- 1 ea bay leaf

Infused olive oil

- 2 cups extra virgin olive oil
- 6 sprigs rosemary
- 6 sprigs fresh thyme
- 8 ea whole black peppercorns
- 4 ea dried juniper berries
- 2 ea bay leaves
- 1 clove garlic, smashed
- 1 tsp chopped parsley
- 1 tsp chopped oregano
- Zest of one lemon

Instructions – marinade

1. Mix all ingredients in a large mixing bowl and set aside.

Instructions – infused oil

1. Combine all ingredients in a glass carafe or "Evian" glass bottle.
2. Allow infusing for 24 to 48 hours prior to service.
3. Refrigerate after 48 hours.

Cooking instructions

1. Brush chicken with olive oil, salt and pepper.
2. Grill on hot side of the grill for 3 minutes a side, turning chicken breasts to create diamond marks.
3. Brush chicken with infused olive oil during grilling.
4. Transfer to carry over side and continue to cook for an additional 4 to 5 minutes until chicken is fully cooked.
5. Brush chicken generously with infused olive oil prior to service.

NOTES

GRILLED SALMON STEAK WITH GRAIN MUSTARD AND HONEY GLAZE

- 2 ea 6 oz salmon steaks
- ¼ cup olive pomace oil
- Salt and pepper to taste

Grain mustard and honey glaze

- 1 cup honey
- ¼ cup course grain Dijon mustard
- 1 TBS Dijon mustard
- 1 TBS lime juice
- 2 TBS chopped parsley
- Salt and pepper to taste

Instructions – glaze

1. Combine all ingredients in a large mixing bowl and mix well.
2. Transfer to a medium saucepan and heat on grill until warm but not boiling.

Cooking instructions

1. Brush salmon with olive oil, salt and pepper.
2. Grill salmon on hot side for 2 minutes a side, turning salmon to create diamond marks.
3. Brush salmon with glaze.
4. Transfer salmon to carry over side and continue to cook for an additional 3 to 4 minutes until desired doneness.
5. Brush generously with glaze prior to serving.

NOTES

_____

_____

_____

_____

_____

_____

_____

_____

_____

_____

_____

_____

_____

_____

_____

_____

_____

_____

_____

_____

_____

_____

GRILLED MARINATED FLANK STEAK

- 1 ea 12 oz flank steak or London broil
- ¼ cup olive pomace oil
- Salt and pepper to taste

Marinade

- 1 cup olive pomace oil
- 1 tsp chopped garlic
- 1 ea chopped shallot
- 1 tsp chopped thyme
- 1 tsp chopped rosemary
- 1 tsp chopped oregano
- 2 TBS Worcestershire sauce
- 1 tsp fresh cracked black pepper
- 1 bay leaf

Instructions – marinade

1. Combine all ingredients in large mixing bowl and mix well.
2. Pour half of marinade onto cookie sheet and place steaks into marinade.
3. Pour the remaining half over steaks.
4. Allow marinating for at least ½ hour, up to 2 hours.

Cooking instructions

1. Pat steaks with paper towel to remove excess marinade prior to grilling.
2. Grill on hot side for 2 minutes a side.

3. Transfer to carry over side and cook for an additional 2 minutes.
4. Remove steaks from grill and allow them to sit for 2 minutes.
5. For service, thinly slice flank steaks width wise and serve immediately.

NOTES

SAUTÉED MUSHROOMS AND ONIONS

- 1 cup olive pomace oil
- 1 large onion julienned
- 3 cups sliced button mushrooms
- 1 TBS chopped garlic
- ¼ cup white wine
- 1 tsp Worcestershire sauce
- 1 TBS chopped thyme
- 1 TBS whole butter
- Salt and pepper to taste

Anything grilled always goes better with sautéed mushrooms and onions. This is a good little add-on to anything from your chicken breast, steaks, seafood, whatever you want to serve it with. Also, this can be done simultaneously on the grill while your product is cooking. Your date will be impressed if you can not only cook, but also multi-task.

Instructions

1. Heat large sauté pan on grill.
2. Add olive oil and allow heating for 1 minute.
3. Add onions and cook for 4 to 5 minutes until translucent and beginning to brown.
4. Add garlic.
5. Add mushrooms and continue to cook, 5 to 6 minutes.
6. Add wine and Worcestershire sauce and mix well, letting cook for an additional 1 minute.
7. Finish by adding thyme, butter, and salt and pepper.
8. Keep warm for service.

NOTES

_____

_____

_____

_____

_____

_____

_____

_____

_____

_____

_____

_____

_____

_____

_____

_____

_____

_____

_____

_____

_____

BLENDER DRINKS

Several years ago I was renting a condo, and it was on the first floor bordering the community pool. The view from my *lanai* or porch was just that – quite a view. All of the girls were always lying in the sun. A friend of mine, being Italian, said to me jokingly, "Kid – go get greased down, put on some gold chains, and walk out there with a blender full of blender drinks!" We laughed like hell for about five minutes.

So from that point on, the term we use for frozen drinks is "blender" drinks. A frozen margarita or piña colada is the perfect accompaniment to lazy afternoons by the pool. I'm going to give you the classics. You can't go wrong with the classics. Feel free to add berries or fruits or whatever you want to them. These are the navy blue blazers – or "must-haves" of frozen drinks.

MARGARITA

- 2 TBS kosher salt
- 1 lime wedge
- 3 oz white tequila
- 1 oz triple sec
- 1 oz lime juice
- 1 cup crushed ice

Instructions

1. Pour salt into a saucer.
2. Rub rim of glass with lime wedge and dip in salt to coat the rim thoroughly.
3. Add tequila, triple sec, lime juice, and ice to blender and blend well at high speed.

Add fresh raspberries or strawberries for a variation.

PIÑA COLADA

- 1 ½ oz light rum
- 2 oz coco Lopez cream of coconut
- 2 oz pineapple juice
- 1 cup crushed ice

Instructions

1. Pour rum, cream of coconut, pineapple juice, and ice into a blender.
2. Blend until smooth.
3. Serve with a slice of fresh pineapple and a maraschino cherry garnish.

RUM RUNNER

- 2 cups ice
- 1 oz pine apple juice
- 1 oz orange juice
- 1 oz black berry liquor
- 1 oz banana liquor
- 1 oz light rum
- 1 oz dark rum or aged rum
- Splash of grenadine
- 1 oz Bacardi 151 to float on top (optional)
- Orange slice (garnish)

Instructions

1. Pour ice into blender.
2. Pour all liquid ingredients over ice.
3. Blend until smooth
4. Garnish glass with orange slice and 151 floater

DAIQUIRI

- 1 ½ oz light rum
- 1 TBS triple sec
- 1 ½ oz lime juice
- 1 tsp sugar
- 1 cup crushed ice
- 1 maraschino cherry (garnish)

Instructions

1. Add all ingredients to blender and blend on low for 5 seconds.
2. Then blend on high until firm.

This is the classic Daiquiri recipe. To this recipe you can add a number of things.

- Add 1 banana, 1 oz banana liquor for Banana Daiquiri
- Add ½ cup fresh strawberries, 1/3 cup cranberry juice for strawberry Daiquiri
- Add 1 cup raspberries, ½ oz raspberry vodka for Raspberry Daiquiri

MUDSLIDE

- 2 oz vodka
- 2 oz coffee liquor
- 2 oz Bailey's Irish Cream
- 6 oz scoop vanilla ice cream
- Whipped cream
- Chocolate syrup (garnish)

Instructions

1. Blend all ingredients together except the chocolate syrup.
2. Pour into glass; garnish the top with whipped cream and chocolate syrup.

CHAPTER 8: HEALTH AND FITNESS

"Let's go to my place after spin class — I'll cook for you — or perhaps one of my famous smoothies…" first-date game plan.

WHEN YOU WANT TO STEP UP and present a delicious dinner that appeals to the girl who's health-conscious, here's the *"Let's go to my place after spin class – I'll cook for you – or perhaps one of my famous smoothies…"* first-date game plan.

Staying active and being fit is a big part of today. It's important to be knowledgeable when it comes to eating healthy, because it is likely that any woman you approach is going to be health conscious and physically fit. You wouldn't be attracted to her if she weren't. Having the ability to prepare tasty health-conscious meals is a valuable skill.

The tough part is that "diet" food doesn't taste good. There's no fat. Fat is what gives food flavor. But there is a delicious solution. To provide flavor we'll use ingredients like lemon juice, lime juice, fresh herbs, and olive oil instead of cream and butter and other saturated fats.

When you have the ability to cook healthy, it shows a commitment to your body and a responsibility to your health.

The five keys to staying fit are:

- 20% Strength training
- 20% Cardiovascular training
- 20% Diet
- 20% Supplementation
- 20% Rest/Recovery

The five keys are all equally important, each representing 20% of the whole picture. One is not more important than another. Each component requires 100% effort. Diet and rest/recovery go hand in hand. It's important to give your body the nutrition it needs to adapt to the physical stress. This is called the "Training Effect."

The human body is a remarkable thing. We have the ability to adapt and get stronger based on the demands imposed on it. For instance, if you're constantly writing with a pencil, your finger will develop a callus. This is the Training Effect. It's your body saying, "If I'm going to constantly have this stress on my finger, I better develop a callus to protect myself and get stronger."

This is just like strength training. If you're going to go to the gym and working out, your body's response is to grow stronger. Your body better prepares itself for these demands.

Your body cannot do this without the proper nutrition. The number one component of proper nutrition is protein. Protein is composed of B vitamins. B vitamins are composed of amino acids. Amino acids (Branch chain and non-essential) are responsible for every function in the human body. Protein rebuilds muscle and helps them grow stronger.

For any athlete, it's important to supplement your diet with protein. A great way to do this is through a protein smoothie. For an active adult, you should supplement with 1 gram of protein for every pound of lean body mass. This means if you're 150 lbs and have 10% body fat, you should be taking in at least 135 grams of protein daily, 135 representing the weight of your lean working body mass, minus the 10% body fat.

The post-work out protein smoothie is healthy, easy, and again shows a responsibility to your health. And, she will love it.

Here's a collection of can't-miss recipes that are healthy and easy to prepare.

ROASTED YELLOW FIN TUNA SALAD WITH CAPERS, TOMATOES, AND FRESH HERBS

- 8 oz center-cut yellow fin tuna loin, roasted and then chopped
- ½ cup diced Roma tomatoes, seeded
- 2 TBS capers
- 1 TBS chopped thyme
- 1 TBS chopped oregano
- 1 TBS chopped parsley
- ½ cup extra virgin olive oil
- 2 TBS white balsamic vinegar
- Juice of 1 lemon
- Salt and pepper to taste

Instructions

1. Brush tuna steak with olive oil, and roast in a 350-degree oven for 8 to 10 minutes until done.
2. Allow the tuna to cool completely before chopping.
3. Add all ingredients to a large mixing bowl and mix well.
4. Allow the salad to set up in refrigerator for at least ½ hour prior to service.
5. Serve as a salad with crostinis, crackers, or flat bread crisps, or serve as a sandwich on crusty French or Italian bread.

NOTES

MEDITERRANEAN TABOULI SALAD

o   Pronounced *TAB-BOOL-LEE*

- 1 cup bulgur wheat
- 2 cups boiling water
- 1 shallot, finely minced
- ¼ tsp finely chopped garlic
- ¼ cup extra virgin olive oil
- ½ cup Roma tomatoes, seeded and diced
- ¼ cup chopped mint
- ¼ cup chopped parsley
- 2 TBS lemon juice
- Salt and pepper to taste

Instructions

1. Pour dry bulgur wheat in a large mixing bowl.
2. Pour boiling water over the top of bulgur wheat, and mix well.
3. Cover bowl with plastic wrap and set aside for 10 minutes.
4. Fluff bulgur wheat with a fork to separate kernels, add remaining ingredients, and mix well.
5. Salt and pepper to taste.

NOTES

_____

_____

_____

_____

_____

_____

_____

_____

_____

_____

_____

_____

_____

_____

_____

_____

_____

_____

_____

POLENTA PIZZA WITH TOMATOES, BASIL, CARAMELIZED ONIONS, AND GORGONZOLA CHEESE

- 1 cup polenta meal (coarse ground corn meal)
- 2 ¼ cups boiling water
- 1 tsp salt
- ½ tsp black pepper
- ½ cup olive pomace oil
- 2 cups diced Roma tomatoes
- 2 cups julienned onion
- ½ cup basil chiffonade (cut into thin strips)
- 1 cup crumbled Gorgonzola cheese (Italian blue cheese)

Instructions

1. Boil water in a medium saucepan.
2. Add salt and pepper to water.
3. Slowly add polenta, reduce heat to medium / low, and stir constantly.
4. Cook polenta for 3 to 5 minutes.
5. When cooked, spread polenta evenly on a greased cookie sheet (6"x9") and allow cooling so it firms.
6. Sauté onion in olive oil for 10 to 12 minutes over medium heat, until it begins to brown, or "caramelize."
7. Spread caramelized onion over the top of cooled polenta along with the crumbled Gorgonzola cheese.
8. Bake in a 350-degree oven for 8 to 10 minutes until cheese is melted and begins to brown.
9. To serve, add diced tomatoes and basil to the top and serve immediately.

NOTES

_____

_____

_____

_____

_____

_____

_____

_____

_____

_____

_____

_____

_____

_____

_____

_____

_____

_____

_____

_____

CARROT AND COCONUT SOUP WITH CILANTRO

- ½ cup olive pomace oil
- 2 cups carrots, peeled and chopped
- ¼ cup chopped onion
- ¾ cup sweet potato, peeled and chopped
- 1 TBS chopped garlic
- 3 ½ cups water or chicken broth
- 1ea 8oz can coconut milk
- Salt and pepper to taste
- ½ cup shredded toasted coconut
- ¼ cup chopped cilantro

Instructions

1. Heat large saucepan over medium heat for 1 minute.
2. Add olive oil and onion and sauté for 2 minutes.
3. Add garlic, carrot, and sweet potato, stir for 20 seconds.
4. Add chicken stock or water and simmer for 15 minutes on a medium to light boil.
5. Add coconut milk, simmer for 5 minutes, and pull from heat. Let stand for 5 minutes.
6. Blend soup in blender in small batches, and return puréed soup to sauce pan while passing it through a strainer.
7. Season with salt and pepper.
8. To serve, garnish with cilantro and shredded toasted coconut.

NOTES

_____

_____

_____

_____

_____

_____

_____

_____

_____

_____

_____

_____

_____

_____

_____

_____

_____

_____

_____

_____

_____

_____

GRILLED CHICKEN BREAST OVER FIELD GREENS WITH ROASTED BEETS AND WHITE BALSAMIC VINEGAR

- 2 ea 6 oz boneless skinless chicken breasts

Marinade

- 1 cup olive pomace oil
- 1 ea chopped shallot
- 1 ea chopped garlic clove
- 1 TSB chopped thyme
- 1 TSB chopped rosemary
- 1 TSB cracked black pepper

Salad

- 2 ea red beets, washed and patted dry
- 2 ½ cups mixed field greens
- 1 cup extra virgin olive oil
- Salt and pepper to taste
- ½ cup white balsamic vinegar
- ½ cup chopped fresh herbs (parsley, thyme, oregano, rosemary)

Instructions – chicken

1. Combine all ingredients for the marinade.
2. Marinate chicken breasts for at least ½ hour in marinade.

3. Grill chicken breasts for 8 to 10 minutes until cooked, 4 minutes per side.

Instructions – salad

1. Wash beets under cold water and pat dry.
2. Coat beets with olive oil, salt and pepper, and wrap in aluminum foil.
3. Roast beets in a 350-degree oven for 25 minutes or until beets are tender to the touch.
4. Cool beets in the refrigerator, and peel with a paring knife.
5. Dice beets into ¼ inch dice and set aside.
6. Combine olive oil, vinegar, and fresh herbs and mix well.

To serve

1. Toss greens in balsamic dressing and place in center of plate.
2. Arrange diced roasted beets around the greens and over the top.
3. Slice chicken breasts and place over top.
4. Finish with a little more balsamic dressing over chicken, serve immediately.

NOTES

BROILED SALMON WITH MINTED MELON RELISH

- 2 ea 6 oz salmon steaks
- ¼ cup extra virgin olive oil
- 1 TBS lemon juice
- 1 TBS chopped parsley
- Salt and pepper to taste
- ½ cup diced cantaloupe, ¼ inch dice
- ½ cup diced honeydew melon
- 1 ea kiwi, peeled and diced ¼ inch
- 3 ea strawberries, stemmed and diced ¼ inch
- 1 TBS lime juice
- ½ cup chopped fresh mint

Instructions – salmon

1. Combine olive oil, lemon juice, parsley and mix well.
2. Brush salmon steaks with olive oil mixture and place on greased cookie sheet.
3. Preheat oven for 5 minutes on "broil" setting.
4. Place cookie sheet with salmon on the bottom rack of oven and broil for 8 to 10 minutes.

Instructions – minted melon relish

1. Peel kiwi by cutting off both ends and sliding a teaspoon just underneath the skin.
2. Run the spoon carefully around the skin to remove in one large piece.

3. Combine all diced fruit and ingredients and mix well.
4. Allow to set up for at least 15 minutes prior to serving.

To serve

1. Spoon a small amount of minted melon relish in center of the plate
2. Place salmon in the middle of the plate, over the top of relish.
3. Spoon melon relish over the top, and around.

NOTES

_____

_____

_____

_____

_____

_____

_____

_____

_____

_____

_____

_____

_____

_____

_____

_____

_____

_____

_____

_____

_____

_____

GRILLED SOUTHWEST SWORDFISH WITH BLACK BEANS AND AVOCADO

- 2 ea 6oz swordfish steaks
- 1 avocado, peeled and diced
- ½ cup olive pomace oil
- 1 tsp ground cumin
- 1 tsp ground coriander
- 1 TBS chopped cilantro
- 1 TBS lime juice
- Salt and pepper

Black beans

- 12 oz can of black beans, drained and rinsed
- ¼ cup olive pomace oil
- ¼ cup diced green pepper
- ¼ cup diced red pepper
- ¼ cup diced onion
- 1 TBS chopped garlic
- 1 cup chicken broth or water
- 1 TBS ground cumin
- 1 TBS ground coriander
- Salt and pepper to taste

Instructions – swordfish

1. Combine olive oil with remaining ingredients and mix well.
2. Rub swordfish with olive oil mixture and allow marinating for at least ½ hour.
3. Grill on hot side of grill for 2 minutes a side.

4. Transfer to carry over side and cook for an additional 3 to 4 minutes.

Instructions, black beans

1. Heat medium size saucepan over medium heat for 1 minute.
2. Add olive oil, peppers, onion, garlic, and dry spices and sauté for 1 minute.
3. Add black beans and cook for an additional 1 minute.
4. Pour liquid over black beans, bring to boil, and then turn heat to low.
5. Allow beans to simmer for 15 minutes on low heat.
6. Liquid should be almost all reduced leaving a thick consistency.
7. Salt and pepper to taste.

To serve

1. Place a generous scoop of black beans in the center of a plate.
2. Serve swordfish over the top.
3. Garnish with freshly diced or sliced avocado.

NOTES

THE FAMOUS SMOOTHIE MENU.

WILD BERRY PROTEIN SMOOTHIE

- ¼ cup raspberries
- ¼ cup blueberries
- 1 cup low fat yogurt
- 1 cup non fat milk
- 1 scoop (35g) whey protein
- ¼ cup wheat germ
- 1 TBS honey

Instructions

1. Add all ingredients to blender.
2. Blend on low for 10 seconds.
3. Blend on high for 45 seconds to 1 minute until smooth.

PEANUT BUTTER AND BANANA SMOOTHIE

- 1 banana
- 2 TBS creamy peanut butter
- 1 TBS honey
- 1 scoop (35g) whey protein
- 1 ½ cups non fat milk
- ¼ cup walnut halves

Instructions

1. Add all ingredients to blender and blend on high until smooth.

TROPICAL FRUIT SMOOTHIE

- ½ cup diced pineapple
- ½ cup diced mango
- ½ cup ice cubes
- ½ cup pineapple juice
- 1 cup low fat yogurt
- 2 TBS shredded coconut
- 1 scoop (35g) whey protein

Instructions

1. Add all ingredients to blender.
2. Blend on low for 10 seconds.
3. Continue to blend on high for 45 seconds or until smooth.

MOCHA CINNAMON DESSERT SMOOTHIE

- 1 cup vanilla flavored frozen yogurt
- ½ cup non fat milk
- 1 scoop (35g) whey protein
- ¼ cup chocolate syrup
- ½ cup chopped hazelnuts
- 1 ½ TBS ground cinnamon
- 1 cup coffee, chilled

Instructions

1. Add all ingredients to blender, blend on low for 10 seconds.
2. Continue to blend on high until smooth.

SUPER SOY PROTEIN SMOOTHIE

- 1 cup soy milk, vanilla
- 2 scoops soy protein powder (25g)
- ½ cup wheat germ

For extra flavor add fresh berries or fruit.

Instructions

1. Add all ingredients to blender and blend on high until smooth.

CHAPTER 9: BREAKFAST!

"When the first date dinner turns into the 2nd date breakfast..."
First date.

You NEVER KNOW when the first-date dinner leads to the second-date breakfast.

With a little help from this book, my bet is that you're going to have many successful first-date dinners. A little confidence along with some culinary know-how will have you in the driver's seat. What a great feeling to have the confidence to approach a woman, have a plan, and execute it to a "T."

Every so often, the *Single Guy Gods* are going to smile down on you. That first-date dinner is going to translate into the second-date breakfast. Dinner is going to go off without a hitch, then some coffee, dessert, a whole bunch of wine, a lot of laughter, and the end result – a loss of the track of time. At this point, it's probably safer if she just spends the night… I mean, it's a bit risky for her to be driving home and it's awfully late anyways, right?

When this happens, you better be prepared to put together a little breakfast. You have no idea how far this is going to go with her. You throwing together a frittata or French toast in a way that's *casual* and *matter of fact* will knock her socks off – again. The coffee's brewing, you're wearing your pajama pants while you cook, and the juice is already on the table. Open the blinds and let a little light in. Turn the TV off and have some conversation. Make some Bloody Marys. Set the table up on the *lanai* and get some fresh air. Turn this potentially awkward moment into something special.

Whether she would admit or not, she will be blown away.

WHOLE-WHEAT TOAST AND THE PERFECT BLOODY MARY

(when you had a rough night…)

- 2 oz vodka
- 6 oz V8 juice
- 1 tsp horseradish
- 1/2 tsp fresh lime juice
- 4 dashes Tabasco sauce
- 4 dashes Worcestershire sauce
- 1 pinch pepper
- 1 pinch celery salt
- 4 slices whole wheat bread
- 1 stick whole butter

Instructions

1. Add several ice cubes to a highball glass.
2. Grind some pepper on top and add some celery salt to make seasoned ice cubes.
3. Add all ingredients to a cocktail shaker half-filled with ice cubes, and shake well.
4. Strain the mixture over the ice cubes in the highball glass.
5. Squeeze a lime slice over the drink and drop it in the glass.

NOTES

BREAKFAST FRITTATA WITH PEPPERS, ONIONS, AND SLICED TURKEY

- 2 TBS whole butter
- 1 cup julienned turkey
- ¼ cup diced red pepper
- ¼ cup diced green pepper
- ¼ cup diced Spanish onion
- 6 ea large eggs
- 1 tsp chopped thyme
- Salt and pepper to taste

Instructions

1. Heat 9" sauté pan for 1 minute over low heat.
2. Add butter, let heat for 20 seconds
3. Add peppers, onions and sauté for 1 minute.
4. Add turkey and sauté 30 seconds
5. Beat eggs together, season with salt and pepper, add thyme to eggs, and pour into pan.
6. Cook frittata for 2 minutes over medium to low heat without stirring.
7. Finish by cooking in a 325-degree oven for 2 to 3 minutes.

NOTES

HEALTHY GRANOLA WITH MIXED BERRIES

- 4 cups prepared unsweetened granola
- ½ cup raspberries
- ½ cup blueberries
- ½ cup strawberries, cut into quarters
- ¼ cup dried cranberries
- ¼ cup raw sugar
- 1 qt fat free milk or skim milk

Instructions

1. Toss granola with fruit and divide into 2 bowls
2. Pour milk over granola, sprinkle with raw sugar.

NOTES

_____

_____

_____

_____

_____

_____

_____

_____

_____

_____

_____

_____

_____

_____

_____

_____

_____

_____

_____

_____

_____

_____

_____

_____

POACHED EGGS OVER ENGLISH MUFFIN WITH HAM, CHEDDAR, AND SPINACH

- 4 large eggs
- 2 English muffins
- 4 slices ham
- 4 slices mild cheddar cheese
- ½ cup blanched spinach
- 2 TSB white vinegar
- Salt and pepper to taste

Instructions

1. Fill 2-qt sauce pan ¾ full with water and bring to a light boil on stove.
2. Add vinegar to simmering water.
3. Toast English muffins and set aside.
4. Butter English muffin and place ham and spinach on top.
5. Cook eggs in water for 3 to 4 minutes, just until egg whites congeal and yolk begins to harden.
6. Remove eggs with slotted spoon and place 1 egg on each of the English muffins.
7. Season eggs with salt and pepper.
8. Cover eggs with sliced cheddar and melt in preheated oven for 1 minute prior to serving.

NOTES

_____

_____

_____

_____

_____

_____

_____

_____

_____

_____

_____

_____

_____

_____

_____

_____

_____

_____

_____

_____

_____

_____

_____

CLASSIC FRENCH TOAST WITH MACERATED BERRIES

- 3 slices Texas toast or thick-cut white bread
- 3 eggs
- ½ cup whole milk
- 1 TSB vanilla extract
- 1 TBS ground cinnamon
- 1 TSB sugar
- 1 tsp salt
- ¼ cup blueberries
- ¼ cup raspberries
- ¼ cup strawberries cut into quarters
- 1 cup water
- ½ cup sugar
- ¼ cup dark rum

Instructions

1. Mix berries together, and cover with water, sugar and rum.
2. Allow to sit for at least 30 minutes prior to serving.
3. Combine eggs, milk, vanilla, cinnamon, sugar, and salt and mix well.
4. Preheat non-stick frying pan over medium heat.
5. Dip bread into egg mixture, coating both sides and place in pan.
6. Cook over medium to low heat for 30 to 45 seconds until bread is golden brown.
7. Turn toast over and repeat.
8. To serve, cut toast on the diagonal and top with macerated berries, being careful to lift the berries out of the excess liquid.

NOTES

_____

_____

_____

_____

_____

_____

_____

_____

_____

_____

_____

_____

_____

_____

_____

_____

_____

_____

_____

_____

_____

_____

SARATOGA OATMEAL WITH DRIED BERRIES AND HONEY

- 2 cups regular oats
- 4 cups water
- ½ TBS salt
- 1 TSB butter
- ¼ cup dried cranberries
- ¼ cup dried currants
- ¼ cup dried cherries
- 1 TSB sugar
- ½ TSB ground cinnamon
- ½ cup honey

Instructions

1. Heat saucepan on low heat and add butter.
2. Add all mixed berries to butter and cook for 1 minute.
3. Add oats to berries and stir well, cooking for 30 seconds. Pour water over oats, add salt, and simmer over medium heat for 4 to 5 minutes or until water is absorbed.
4. Stir in sugar and cinnamon while cooking.
5. Drizzle honey over oatmeal prior to serving, while still hot.

NOTES

WILD BERRY BREAKFAST SMOOTHIE

- ½ cup raspberries
- ½ cup strawberries
- ½ cup blueberries
- 12 oz plain yogurt
- 1 cup orange juice
- ¼ cup wheat germ
- ¼ cup honey

Instructions

1. Add all ingredients in a blender and blend well.
2. Add more orange juice if not blending properly.

NOTES

CONCLUSION

I HOPE THAT *The Bachelor's Guide to First-Date Cooking* is both inspirational and a practical resource.

I wrote it to be inspirational and to help you to recognize that the skills you possess on the job or in sports or playing poker are no different than the skills you can develop in the kitchen. It's all a matter of confidence and attitude. When you walk into work every day you probably have a winning attitude, and it translates into tangible results. The dating game is no different.

It's a practical resource that you can rely on year after year, like any other technical manual. Once you get comfortable in the kitchen, I encourage you to try your own variations. Add different spices or ingredients and see what you come up with. Remember, stovetop or grill cooking is not like baking, which must be done with absolute precision. The recipes in *The Bachelor's Guide to First-Date Cooking* are flexible and forgiving. If you screw up a recipe the first time, just try again.

Stay tuned for updated editions with more recipes and more information to help you win the dating game. And if you have any comments or suggestions, drop me a line. You can find me at:

http://www.thebachelorsguidetofirstdatecooking.com/

chris@thebachelorsguidetofirstdatecooking.com.

Good luck!

Chris

GLOSSARY

Acrylic finish - A treatment for the exterior surfaces of aluminum or stainless steel; allows for a variety of colors to be applied to the cookware.

Acrylic silkscreen - A decorative process in which a special ink or paste is forced through a design on a screen and bonded to metal at high temperature.

Aged beef - Refers to wholesale beef cuts that are held at refrigerated temperatures for a specified period of time in order to optimize the tenderness and flavor of the product.

Al Dente - Literally, "to the tooth" in Italian. Foods cooked to the point that there is still some resistance; tender, but slightly chewy. Used mostly in reference to pasta.

Allspice - Can be purchased whole or ground. The flavor tastes like a blend of cinnamon, cloves and nutmeg and is widely used in braised meats, pies and puddings.

Aluminum - One of the two principal metals used in cookware; lightweight, excellent conductor of heat and relatively inexpensive.

Amaranth - Like quinoa, amaranth is considered a pseudo cereal (technically not a grain). Amaranth is gluten-free, high in protein, and contains lysine (making it a complete protein). Amaranth grains can be cooked whole in a pot, rice cooker, or pressure cooker for a breakfast porridge.

Anasazi beans - Reddish-brown beans with white markings are popular in Southwestern recipes, including soups and refried beans.

Angel food pan - The angel food pan also known as a tube pan is a round, high-sided pan with a hollow cylinder in the center that provides the traditional angel food cake shape.

Angus beef cattle - Angus cattle comprises two breeds of hornless cattle from the original Scottish Aberdeen stock, Black Angus and Red Angus (the original name of the breed was Aberdeen Angus). Black is the predominant color; Black Angus is the most popular breed for beef in the U.S.

Anise seed - Can be whole or ground and has a nice licorice flavor. It is basically used in Italian sausage but can also be used in pastries, cookies and breads.

Anodized finish - A treatment for aluminum cookware, created by an electrochemical process that increases the thickness of the natural oxide film of aluminum.

Apple corer - An apple corer is an inexpensive utensil that removes the core of an apple while leaving the apple whole.

Baby back ribs - While most people think of baby back ribs (or simply, back ribs) as pork, they are also available from a steer. Also called loin ribs, they come from the top back of the rib cage, where the bones are short ("baby") but meaty. Spare ribs, which come from the front, or belly side, have more fat, but the meat is "spare."

Bakeware - Products used for foods, which cook by absorbing heat from the surrounding hot air, as in an oven.

Baking tray - Large and small, aluminum or stainless steel tray for baking purposes.

Balsamic vinegar - A dark, sweet vinegar, made from reduced white wine, that has been matured in wooden barrels, the resins of which contribute to its flavor; especially such a vinegar from Modena in Italy.

Bamboo steamer - A special kind of steamer made from bamboo strips used especially in Chinese cooking for steaming dimsums.

Barley - Grain with an especially tough hull, which when stripped removes some of the bran. There are hull-less varieties, most commonly found in natural-food stores and by mail order. Barley contains beta-glucan, a soluble fiber attributed to lowering cholesterol, and protein comparable to wheat; it is not gluten-free. Barley is a versatile grain, good in soups, risotto, and grain salads

Basil - Can be fresh or dried. It's an aromatic herb with a sweet smell and flavor. Basil is used in tomato dishes, pasta sauce and great with lamb chops, meat dishes and salads.

Baste - To add moisture, flavor and color to foods by brushing, drizzling or spooning pan juices or other liquids over the food at various times during the cooking process. This is especially essential when cooking with dry heat, such as oven roasting or grilling.

Baster - Used to lift the fat and liquids from the bottom of a roasting pan and then pour that liquid over the meat, keeping the meat moist, adding more flavor, and creating a glaze as it cooks.

Bay leaves - Whole ground leaves with a pungent aroma used basically in soups, stews and braised meats.

Bean - Bean originally meant the seed of the broad bean, but the definition was later expanded to include members of the genus *Phaseolus* such as the common bean or haricot and the runner bean and the related genus *Vigna*, which includes the mung bean, the rice bean and the black-eyed pea. The term is now

THE BACHELOR'S GUIDE TO FIRST DATE COOKING

applied in a general way to some 15 other genuses which include such varieties as soybeans, peas, lentils, chickpea (garbanzo), pea, lentil, lima, common bean (including the black bean, pinto bean and kidney bean), soybean and guar.

Beat - To mix thoroughly with a spoon, whisk or beaters until well-combined and very smooth.

Béchamel sauce - White sauce: milk thickened with a butter and flour roux.

Beef - The culinary name for meat from bovines, especially domestic cattle, although beef also refers to the meat from the other bovines: antelope, African buffalo, bison, water buffalo and yak.

Beef jerky - One of the oldest ways of preserving food; meat was cut into strips, smoked and dried in the sun. Today it is smoked and dried in smokers.

Bisque - A smooth, creamy, highly seasoned soup of French origin, classically based on a strained broth (coulis) of crustaceans. It can be made from lobster, crab, shrimp or crayfish. Also, creamy soups made from roasted and puréed vegetables are sometimes called bisques.

Black Bean (a.k.a. black Spanish bean, common bean, tampico bean, turtle bean, Spanish bean or Venezuelan bean) - A relative of the kidney bean, the black bean (*Phaseolus vulgaris*) are small, kidney-shaped and shiny. Black beans hold their shape when cooked and absorb flavors well.

Black-eyed pea (*Vigna unguiculata*) - Medium-sized (3/8 inch long), ivory-colored beans with a large black coloration (the "eye") on the inner curve of the beans. They are commonly used in bean cakes, casseroles, curry dishes, fritters and salads. Variations are yellow, brown or red in color.

Blade Steak - The blade steak is cut from the chuck. The cut is not popular because it has a line of tough connective tissue down its center, resulting in a tough steak best suited to braising. However, if the tissue is removed, it produces flat iron steaks, a more tasty, value priced cut.

Blanche - To partially cook food, usually vegetables or fruit, in boiling water or steam. Immediately after blanching, vegetables are usually placed in ice water to stop the cooking and set the color.

Blend - To mix ingredients just until thoroughly combined. Not originally meant to be prepared in a blender, but can be in some recipes.

Blender - Excellent for mixing drinks, grinding spices, puréeing foods and making smooth sauces.

Boil - To heat liquids until bubbles form on the surface, and then to keep it at that temperature during the cooking process.

Boning knife - A type of kitchen knife with a sharp point and narrow blade. It is used in food preparation for removing the bones of poultry, meat, and fish, generally 12 cm to 17 cm (5 to 6 ½ inches) in length.

Box grater - This grater is different from your regular flat grater. It can handle a variety of foods, from cinnamon to chocolate, cheese to vegetables.

Braise - To cook slowly in a small amount of liquid in a covered pot. Foods are usually browned prior to braising to add flavor. Braising can be done on top of the stove or in an oven, depending on the recipe.

Brie - A soft cows' cheese named after Brie, the French province in which it originated (roughly corresponding to the modern département of Seine-et-Marne). It is pale in colour with a slight greyish tinge under crusty white mould; very soft and savoury.

Brown - Generally, when a recipe says to "brown," it refers to cooking quickly in a hot pan, on the grill or under a broiler until all sides turn golden or brown in color. The purpose is to seal in the juices and add flavor.

Bruschetta - An appetizer whose origin dates to at least the 15th century from central Italy. It consists of grilled bread rubbed with garlic and topped with extra-virgin olive oil, salt and pepper, and whatever toppings so chosen.

Butterfly - A method of cutting meats so that it will lay flat and even. Difficult to describe without visual effects, but the meat is sliced in the center, without going all the way through, and opened to lay flat like the wings of a butterfly. In larger cuts, it is sliced in increments from middle to either side, and the flaps are opened like the pages of a book.

Cake comb - This triangular metal or plastic tool with saw-tooth edges is used to make patterns in frosting.

Cake Tester - A long wire used to test cakes for doneness. Wooden toothpicks can also be used in place of a cake tester.

Cannellini bean - A glossy white, oval bean with a thin skin and mild flavor.

Canola oil - This is the market name for "rapeseed oil," Canada's most widely used oil. Also called lear oil, for "low erucic acid rapeseed" oil. Canola oil is lowest in saturated fat of any oil. Canola oil is 6% saturated fat; palm oil is 79%.

Capacities - Liquid measurements; measured at full level, except where otherwise noted. Allowable manufacturing tolerance is plus or minus 5 percent of total volume.

Capers - From the flower buds of the caper bush, these salty berries are a fantastic addition to fish dishes and salads as well as pasta.

Caramelize - The process through which natural sugars in foods become browned and flavorful while cooking. This is usually done over a constant heat of low to medium-low. Caramelization can be quickened with the addition of a little sugar. Either way, be careful not to burn.

Caraway seed - Whole and is a widely familiar flavor in rye breads but may also be used in sauerkraut, cheese spreads and pork.

Cardamom - May be whole or ground. These tiny brown seeds are sweet and aromatic and may be used for pickling, pastries and curries.

Carving board - Usually made of hardwood and similar to a cutting board, but it has a "gutter" around the edges or down the center to catch meat juices.

Casserole dish - A thick-walled (usually cast iron) cooking pot with a tight-fitting lid. Dutch ovens have been used as cooking vessels for hundreds of years. A large deep dish in which food can be cooked and served.

Cast aluminum - The result of molten aluminum being poured into molds made in the shape of cookware.

Cast iron - One of the oldest materials used in cookware; made from molten alloys, often covered with porcelain exterior and interior finishes.

Cast iron pot - A type of cookware constructed of a heavy metal material known as cast iron, which is a good material for cooking foods. Cast iron absorbs heat well, retaining the warmth and distributing it evenly across the length and width of the cookware.

Cayenne - Ground and very hot. It can be used to spice up sauces, meat of fish,

Celery seed - Whole or ground with a strong celery flavor and used in salads and salad dressings.

Certified Angus Beef® - Certified Angus Beef is a trademarked brand that licenses the trademark to ranchers who are approved by the licensor. The brand promises the consumer consistently flavorful, juicy and tender cuts. Less than 8% of beef is Certified Angus Beef. It is the best-known brand; more than 50% of all beef approved through USDA brand certification (i.e., branded beef) is Certified Angus Beef.

Chakla and belan - Chakla is a small marble or wooden platform and belan is the rolling pin usually made of wood. They are used for rolling doughs.

Chervil - Crushed leaves similar in flavor to parsley or tarragon. Chervil can be used in soups, salads and sauces.

Chiffonade - Finely shredded vegetables, usually herbs, and most often to be used as a garnish.

Chili powder - Ground blended spice of cumin, chili peppers, garlic and oregano and mainly used in Mexican dishes.

Chives - Can be either fresh or dried herb with a slight onion flavor and used in a variety of fish, meat and vegetable dishes.

Chop - To cut foods into small pieces. Sizes vary from fine (approximately 1/4-inch pieces) to coarse (approximately 3/4-inch pieces). In most recipes, precision is not necessary.

Chopping board - It is made of food grade fiber for the purpose of cutting and chopping food items on it.

Chrome-plate - A finish created by a three-step electrolytic process, in which copper, nickel chromium are applied to a steel core.

Chuck - (a.k.a. shoulder cuts) There are more than a half dozen cuts from the shoulder (the area between the neck and the shoulder blade) including arm steak, blade steak, chuck steak, chuck eye steak, mock tender steak, seven bone steak, shoulder steak and under bone steak. All of them have excellent flavor, but they are usually tougher than cuts from the loin, sirloin or rib sections, and are thus less expensive. These multi-muscled steaks are best cooked by braising.

Chuck steak - An extremely well marbled, full-bodied and robust steak. The typical chuck steak is a rectangular cut, cut about one-inch thick, with parts of the shoulder bones, and is known as a "7-bone steak." This is a reference to the shape of the bone, which resembles the numeral 7. From a good producer, this can be a very satisfying cut.

Ciabatta bread - An Italian white bread made with wheat flour and yeast. The loaf is somewhat elongated, broad and flattish and, like a slipper, should be somewhat collapsed in the middle

Cinnamon - An aromatic bark used in hams, sweet potatoes and hot beverages.

Clad - Usually refers to the bonding of one metal to another, such as copper to stainless steel, in a way that takes advantage of the characteristics of both metals.

Clarify - To make a liquid clear, as with butter. Unsalted butter is melted over low heat until the milk solids come to the top. They are then removed. Without the milk solids, the butter may be used in recipes in which you don't want it to brown.

Cling film - A transparent food grade ultra thin plastic sheet used for covering cooked, uncooked food kept in food trays, bowls etc.

Cloves - Either whole of ground with a pungent sweet flavor basically used in hams, marinades, stocks and braised meats.

Coddle - To cook gently just below the boiling point. Most commonly refers to eggs, where the egg is cooked for 1 minute in the shell.

Colander - Round, deep utensil with lots of holes meant to drain liquid and retain the residue for further processing.

Congeal - To turn liquid into solid by chilling.

Conical strainer - This cookware cooking utensil is similar to the colander (see above), this, as the name suggests is a conical shaped device containing very small holes which is generally used to remove lumps from sauces.

Cookie cutter - Cookie cutters of metal or plastic cut round, square or decorative shapes from cookie dough.

Cookie press - A tube that is filled with cookie dough and a mechanism that pushes the dough through decorative disks.

Cookie sheet - A wide, flat metal pan suitable for baking in an oven.

Cooking spoon - A kitchen utensil that is used for several purposes, such as stirring, serving and transferring food. It has a bowl shaped head attached to a handle.

Cooling rack - A cooling rack is a raised wire rack used to cool baked goods. It is raised to allow air circulation around the baking pan, which hastens cooling and prevents steam accumulation.

Copper - The metal's ability to conduct heat evenly makes it especially effective for top-of-range cooking.

Coriander - Whole or ground spice with a slightly sweet musty flavor. it can be used for pickling, sausages, pork or curried dishes.

Corn-fed - (or grain-fed) cattle that eat a diet of corn. In addition to being unhealthy for the animal, it creates a fattier meat than the leaner, grass-fed beef.

Corned beef - Corning refers to curing or pickling the meat in a seasoned brine. The word refers to the "corns" or grains of kosher (or other coarse) salt that is mixed with water to make the brine. Typically, brisket is used to make corned beef.

Couplers - A grooved insert and ring for the decorating bags that allows tip changes without changing bags. The coupler has two parts; the inner coupler base and the outer coupler ring.

Couscous - Pronounced KOOS-koos, this wheat product is more than 1,000 years old. It's not a grain but yellow granules of semolina, made from durum pasta wheat, which are precooked and then dried. Like pasta or rice, couscous is versatile and has numerous preparations. It is simple to prepare: Just add boiling water and let it sit.

Cowboy steak - A cowboy steak is a bone-in rib steak with a Frenched rib bone. This "raw bone" feature and the fact that this cut is generally around two pounds of meat, makes it big enough for the hungriest cowboy.

Cracked wheat (Bulgur) - Cracked wheat and bulgur are one and the same: wheat kernels that have been precooked, dried, and cut ("cracked"). This processing is what makes bulgur such a convenience food when it comes to preparing whole grains; it takes minimal time (boiling or soaking) to make it tender. High in fiber, bulgur is not gluten-free. It makes great salads, pilafs, and side dishes; substitute bulgur for rice if you're short on time, as an accompaniment to stir-fries, curries, or stews.

Cream - To beat an ingredient or ingredients with a spoon or beaters until light and fluffy. Most often used in reference to butter or shortening, with or without sugar, in baking recipes.

Cube - Cut into squares, size of which is determined by the recipe, generally between 1/2 to 2-inches.

Cumin seed - A small seed that looks like caraway and is used in chili powder, sausages and meats.

Cut in - To work a solid fat, such as butter, shortening or lard, into dry ingredients. This is accomplished by using a pastry blender, 2 knives, a fork, or even the fingers. Most often, the fat should be chilled first and "cut in" just enough for small lumps about the size of a pea to form.

Cutlery - Machine-made knives using less craftsmanship than forged cutlery. Usually does not include a metal bolster, and may also be referred to as "cold pressed" cutlery.

Dash - If a recipe calls for "a dash" of an ingredient, it is somewhat relative. However, the most accurate amount appears to be 1/16-teaspoon. Basically, you just add the ingredient "in a dash."

Debone - To remove the bones from meat or poultry. This is best done with a flexible boning knife so that you can get as close to the bone as possible without losing meat. If in doubt, get a good cookbook that shows the process in stages, or watch a good, informative cooking show. Your butcher will also do it for you, but it's fun to learn how.

Decorating bags - Decorating bags are lightweight, flexible, reinforced for strength and can be reused. Decorating bags are made of either polyester or disposable plastic.

Deep fry - To fry foods rapidly in a deep pot of oil so that the food is totally submerged. The oil should never come up much more than half way in the pot, and should be a type with a high smoking point.

Deglaze - The process of scraping up all the fond or browned bits that collects in the bottom of a pan or skillet after cooking. Liquid is added to the pan and, as it heats up, the bottom is scraped with a spoon or spatula so that the residue is added back into the liquid for lots of extra flavor.

Demitasse spoon - Ideal for serving coffee, tea or other after dinner refreshments.

Dice - To cut into very small pieces, approximately 1/8 to 1/16-inch.

Dill seed - Can be purchased whole or crushed and has a dill pickle flavor and is widely used for pickling, soups, salads and fish.

Dough scraper - A dough scraper is a rectangular implement, usually with a wooden handle and a metal blade. It is used for loosening and turning dough and for scraping excess dough from the work surface.

Dredge - To coat before cooking with dry ingredients such flour, corn meal, bread or cracker crumbs, or other mixtures

Dry-aged - Fresh beef that has been hung to dry (or set on wooden racks) in an aging room for several weeks under controlled temperatures, humidity and air flow to reduce spoilage and enhance flavor and tenderness. It is compared to aged wine: The flavors have deepened and mellowed. Only the more expensive cuts of meat can be dry-aged, as the process requires meat with a large, evenly distributed fat content.

Dust - To sprinkle lightly before or after cooking with dry ingredients, such as flour, granulated or confectioner's sugar or spices.

Edamame - The cooked green soybean is very popular as a snack, squeezed from the pod. It is also served as a side dish and used as an accent in casseroles, salads, soups, and rice and pasta dishes.

Egg slicer - An egg slicer is a tool designed to cut perfect slices of hard-cooked eggs with thin wires.

Emulsify - To bind together liquid ingredients that do not dissolve into each other. Most common is oil into vinegar or citrus juice to make a vinaigrette, or clarified butter into egg yolks to make Hollandaise sauce. The oil is poured very slowly into the acid while whisking or blending vigorously, until the mixture is thickened and the liquids become one.

Espagnole sauce - A rich brown sauce thickened with roux, made with veal stock, and usually tomato product added to stock.

Extra virgin olive oil - Processed from ripened olives, the extra virgin oil type is taken from the first press, which tends to be the most flavorful.

Eye of round roast - The leanest of all roasts and the most tender of roasts from the round, there is virtually no exterior fat. Just season and roast this cut for 20 minutes per pound at 300°F. It also does well cooked in warm moist heat such as a crock pot.

Fava bean - (a.k.a. Broad bean, faba or horse bean) The Fava bean (*Vica faba*) is a flat, oval bean, 3/4 to 1 inch in length, housed in a large, green, inedible pod. It has an assertive, almost bitter earthy flavor and granular texture.

Fennel seed - Has a distinct licorice flavor used in sausage, tomato sauces and fish.

Feta (φέτα) - A brined curd cheese traditionally made in Greece. A sheep's milk cheese, varying amounts of goats' milk may be added, as long as goat milk makes up less than 30% of the total mixture. Since 2005, feta has been a protected designation of origin product in the European Union.

Fillet - To remove bones from a fish, so that only the flesh remains. The process depends on the type of fish. Though similar, it is different for flat fish, like a flounder, or round fish, like a trout.

Fish spatula - The term given to a flat spatula that has long open spaces within the spatula, as to pick fish out of the pan and leave behind any grease or oil.

Flageolet beans - Small beans that can be found in black, green, red, white and yellow varieties. Flageolets, about a half-inch in length, are often mistaken for small kidney beans.

Flake - To gently separate into small pieces, usually with a fork or your fingers. Most commonly refers to cooked fish which, because of its texture, flakes easily.

Flank steak - (London broil) The long, triangular-shaped muscle from the fibrous underside of a flank of beef. A traditional preparation is marinated, broiled rare and sliced thin against the grain of the beef (London broil is a misnomer, as the dish did not originate in London). Flank steaks, along with sirloin steaks, have a robust, beefy flavor, but they are substantially tougher. Thus, they are generally marinated or cooked using a moist method such as braising. They also can be rolled and stuffed, then baked in the oven or cooked in a crockpot.

Flatiron steak - A relatively new cut from the shoulder, a major barrier to prior enjoyment was the large band of connective tissue running down the center of the steak. This led people to assume that the cut in general must be tough. Removing the connective tissue leads to a steak that is often described as having both the tenderness of rib eye or strip steak while still having the earthy flavor of a sirloin or skirt steak. Most people marinate the cut.

Flite mignon - The most expensive cut of beef comes from the small end of the tenderloin. Boneless, it is ideally 2-1/2 inches thick (although it is sliced thinner) and 1-1/2 to 3 inches in diameter. Because this area of the animal is not weight-bearing, the connective tissue is not toughened by exercise. This results in extremely tender meat, the most tender of all beef cuts. It is lightly marbled and mild flavored compared to other cuts. The term "filet mignon" is a French derivative; the literal meaning is small (mignon) boneless meat (filet). On restaurant menus it is called Filet Mignon, Tournedos, Medallions, Filet de Boeuf, and Tenderloin Steak.

Fold - To gently mix two or more ingredients together, where one is usually heavier than the other, in order to combine but preserve the texture of each. For example, to combine whipped cream or beaten egg whites with a heavy batter without deflating. First, stir a little of the whipped product into the batter to lighten it. Then add the remainder. Cut through the center with a rubber spatula, move across the bottom of the bowl towards the side, and gently bring up some of the heavy mixture. Continue, turning the bowl slightly each time, until combined. It is acceptable to leave a few streaks of egg whites when beating them into a batter.

Fondue - From the French "fonder," which means to melt. A dish of warm, melted cheese flavored with wine, into which bits of bread are dipped.

Food processor - An electric equipment run by motor used to break down food items or for blending and other purposes.

French knife - Also known as a chef's knife is a cutting tool used in food preparation. The chef's knife is an evolution of the butcher knife, and was originally designed primarily to slice and disjoint large cuts of beef. Now, it's the primary knife of the kitchen with a wide blade at the handle, and gradually narrowing down towards the tip.

Frenched - A sophisticated and elegant presentation where the meat is removed from the bottom portion of the bone. It makes a roast easier to carve as well.

Frittata - A type of Italian omelet either simple or enriched with additional ingredients, such as meats, cheeses, vegetables and even pasta. It may be compared to a crust-less quiche or, in America, "scrambled eggs." A frittata is prepared in a frying pan like a traditional French omelet.

Fry - To cook and brown food in a specified amount fat, usually done very quickly so that a minimal amount of the fat is absorbed into the food.

Frying pan - A shallow thick bottom pan used for shallow frying.

Garbanzo bean (a.k.a. ceci or chickpea) - Small, hard, knobby beans, a rich beige-yellow color, about 3/8 inches round. While high in carbohydrate, their nutty flavor, minimal fat, nutrition (they are a good source of calcium, B vitamins, protein and iron) and versatile culinary qualities have pushed garbanzos to the forefront.

Garlic - Best fresh and has a strong aromatic flavor used in a wide variety of dishes.

Garlic press - A quick and easy tool that presses a clove of garlic in place of fine chopping.

Garnish - To enhance finished foods with flavor or visual appeal by using other edible products on the plate. The most common are herbs, but there are many other possibilities including, but not limited to, fruits, small vegetables and edible flowers.

Gauge - A term used to describe the thickness of aluminum utensils. Gauge usually is described by a number.

Ginger - Can be whole or ground and used in baked goods, desserts and braised meats.

Glaze - The process of dipping or brushing, usually with a sugar-based liquid, to give flavor and a shiny finish to foods, such as roasted or grilled meats, fried pastries or baked goods.

Gorgonzola - A veined Italian blue cheese, made from unskimmed cow's and/or goat's milk. It can be buttery or firm, crumbly and quite salty, with a 'bite' from its blue veining.

Grade A - USDA designation that indicates quality or yield of meat.

Grain mustard - A medium-strength mustard made from mustard seeds blended with vinegar and oil. A great all-rounder for steak and dressings, Grain mustard refers to Dijon mustard with grainy bits of mustard seed left in.

Grate - To rub foods, such as cheeses, vegetables, citrus skins, spices or chocolate, against a grater. Alternately, you can use a processor or mixer blade. Size of grate is dependent upon recipe and/or taste.

Great northern bean - A mild, white, oval bean, similar to the white kidney bean.

Grill pan - A piece of cookware that is used to grill foods. Typically a heavy metal pan containing ridges spaced evenly across the bottom, the grill pan is built to closely simulate the grilling process for cooking various meats and foods.

Grind - To process foods finely in a grinder, processor or with 2 knives (in a drum roll fashion). Some examples are ground beef for hamburgers or ground pork for sausage, but there are preparations other than meats.

Grouper – (pron. GROO-per) Although some weigh 1/3 ton, the average size of this fish is from 5 to 15 pounds. Groupers are found in the waters of the Gulf of Mexico and the waters of the South Pacific. They have a lean, firm flesh that is suitable for baking, broiling, frying, poaching or steaming. The grouper's skin, which is very strongly flavored, should always be removed before cooking. The most popular members of this sea bass family are the black grouper, Nassau grouper, red grouper and yellow mouth (or yellow fin) grouper.

Haddock - White ocean fish similar to cod, with flaky flesh, available fresh or frozen, whole or as steaks and fillets. Can be poached, baked, fried, smoked or grilled and served with or without sauce.

Halibut - A species of fish characterized by its flatness; they are large with a width of about one-third their length. Both eyes are on the top side of the body. Halibut reside on the sandy bottoms of the ocean floor and are harvested by longliners. Their meat is highly valued.

Hollandaise sauce - An emulsion of egg yolk and butter, usually seasoned with lemon juice, salt, and a little white pepper or cayenne pepper. In appearance it is light yellow and opaque, smooth and creamy.

Hummus - A thick spread made from mashed chickpeas, tahini, lemon juice and garlic; used especially as a dip for pita; originated in the Middle East.

IQF - The abbreviation for "Individually Quick Frozen," referring to food that has been first frozen individually, then packaged together.

Julienne - To slice foods in match-size sticks, about 1/8-inch wide and 2-inches long. This can easily be accomplished with a knife by stacking slices, then cutting down very thinly.

Juniper berries - Slightly soft berries that resemble the size and color of blueberries. Pungent, piney flavor, bitter when raw, principle flavoring in gin. Uses: Marinades, game dishes, stocks.

Kidney bean - Familiar to almost every American, these beans find themselves in baked beans, chili, refried beans, three bean salad (along with string beans and wax beans), Cajun bean dishes and stews.

Knead - The process of working a dough to activate the gluten, which is the protein in flour that makes the dough cohesive. To knead by hand, place the dough on a lightly floured surface. Using the heel of the hand, press down on the dough in a forward motion, then fold the dough over and press again. Continue the process until the dough is very smooth and elastic.

Kobe beef - A brand name of Wagyu, named after the Kobe prefecture in Japan, where it is raised.

Kosher salt - A term that describes one of the most commonly used varieties of edible salt in commercial kitchens today. Kosher salt has a much larger grain size than some common table salt allowing for much easier application by hand / fingers, and also is known to not have any additives.

Leaven - To add an ingredient, such as yeast, baking powder or baking soda, that adds gas to a dough or batter, causing it to expand, or rise, and lighten the texture of the finished product.

Lentil - The seed of a small shrub that is dried after harvesting. Lentils have been eaten for over 8,000 years and originated in southwestern Asia along the Indus River. It is a staple food for many South Asian cultures. Tiny, flat and round bean.

Lima bean - (a.k.a. butter bean or Madagascar bean) Among the most popular shell beans in the U.S., these smooth, flat shaped, sweet-tasting beans have a rich, starchy, meaty texture and a creamy, distinctive flavor.

Loaf pan - Loaf pans are used for baking yeast breads, quick breads, loaf-shaped cakes, and meat loaf.

Long-grain brown rice - Brown rice is rice with the germ and bran intact, making it rich in fiber, minerals, and vitamins. (White rice is brown rice that has been polished, which strips the germ, bran, and most of the nutrients.)

Macerate - To add liquid to food, or an ingredient, such as sugar, that causes liquid to form, in order to soften and enhance flavor after it sets for a given amount of time. Usually used in reference to fresh fruits.

Madeira wine - Madeira is a fortified Portuguese wine made in the Madeira Islands. The wine is produced in a variety of styles ranging from dry wines which can be consumed on their own as an aperitif, to sweet wines more usually consumed with dessert.

Mahi mahi - A fish, also known as dolphinfish. Though mahi mahi is a type of dolphin, it is not a mammal. Mahi mahi is a firm, flavorful fish, excellent grilled or broiled

Maître d'hôtel butter - A compound butter made by blending together softened butter, lemon juice or vinegar, chopped parsley and seasonings. It is served as an accompaniment to fish, poultry and meat.

Marble mortar & pestle - A great tool that helps you release the most flavor from herbs and spices. Perfect for grinding herbs, spices and nuts into pastes or powders.

Marinate - To add liquid or dry ingredients to food that enhance flavor and/or tenderize after it sets for a given amount of time, usually used in reference to meats and vegetables. Liquid marinades often include an acid, such as vinegar, wine or citrus juice, mixed with herbs, spices and oil. Dry marinades are usually in the form of spice and herb rubs.

Marjoram - Dried crushed leaves milder in flavor than oregano and used with sauces, poultry, lamb and meats.

Meat mallet - Also called a meat tenderizer, a meat mallet is a hammer like tool that has a head marked with a waffled surface. It flattens the meat while breaking surface fibers.

Melon baller - A melon baller is a small tool that shapes melon into perfect balls. It is also useful for coring apple halves and scooping out cherry tomatoes prior to stuffing.

Metal spatula - Metal spatulas are tools with narrow thin metal blades attached to plastic or wooden handles. They are ideal for spreading.

Metal tongs - Provide you with great control while turning over food items during cooking, or anything else. Makes for safer and easier handling of foods.

Mince - To cut into very fine pieces.

Mint - Aromatic leaves tasting like spearmint or peppermint and mainly used with lamb.

Mix - To combine ingredients with a spoon or beaters until well incorporated.

Mother sauces - As defined by Auguste Escoffier, the five sauces from which all other classic French sauces are derived from - Hollandaise/mayonnaise, Espagnole, Veloute, Béchamel, and tomato sauce.

Muslin cloth - A thin loosely woven cotton cloth used for fine straining purpose such as to drain curds, strain juices or often used to line a sieve.

Mustard seed - Used either whole or ground and has a very strong pungent flavor. It's used in meats, sauces and gravies.

Napa cabbage - This oval-shaped broad-leafed head has very crisp, pale green crinkled leaves and a sweet, delicate flavor. It is used extensively in stir-fried dishes and soups, and absorbs flavors beautifully.

Navy bean - (a.k.a. Yankee bean) a pea-sized, off-white, oval bean, about 3/8-inch long. It is so-named because it has been a staple food for the U.S. Navy since the mid-1800s in soups, pork and beans and other bean dishes (it absorbs flavor easily, so it works well in soups).

New potato - A small, waxy potato that is usually prepared by boiling or steaming and is often eaten with its skin.

New York strip steak - The strip steak is a firm-textured, well-marbled cut, tender, juicy and and flavorful, that is a favorite among steak-eaters (it's the second most popular cut). It comes from the most tender section of beef, the short loin—it is the boneless top loin muscle.

Niçoise - As suggested by the name, it is a specialty of the Cote d'Azur region of France, originating in and named for the city of Nice. Usually any preparation consisting of Niçoise olives, tomatoes, capers, red onion, haricots vert, and sometimes potatoes for the classic dish of salad Niçoise.

Nutmeg - A whole or ground sweet aromatic spice used with soups, vegetables, desserts and pastries.

Oat groats - hulled oat kernels, in their purest form before rolled, steel-cut, or milled into flour. Unlike many grains, oats are rarely processed to remove their germ and bran, making them a whole grain in most permutations.

Olive pomace oil - This oil is extracted from pomace, the pulpy olive residue from which the virgin olive oil has been extracted.

Oregano - Used fresh or dried in many Italian dishes, tomato sauces and meat dishes.

Oxtail - Oxtail was once really from an ox, but today it is usually beef or veal tail. While quite bony and gelatinous meat, is very flavorful, and is popular in British and Caribbean cooking, in stews or soups. Oxtail requires long, slow braising.

Pan fry - To brown and cook foods in fat in a shallow pan, where the fat does not completely cover the food.

Paprika - A ground sweet red pepper with a mild flavor. It's normally used in braised meats and poultry.

Parboil - To partially cook for a given amount of time in boiling water as a preliminary step.

Pare - To remove skins and peels from fruits or vegetables with a small knife or peeler.

Paring knife - A thin-bladed knife intended for coring and paring (peeling) fruit such as apples.

Parma ham - The famous sweet Italian ham which is dry cured and pressed. It is usually eaten raw accompanied by fruit or delicate vegetables. See prosciutto.

Parsley - Best used fresh and has a light sweet flavor used in a wide variety of foods.

Pastry bag - A pastry bag is a cone-shaped bag made of canvas, plastic or plastic-lined cloth. It is used to pipe foods, such as frosting, whipped cream, cream puff dough and mashed potatoes, in a decorative pattern.

Pastry blender - This hand-held tool consists of several u-shaped wires or metal blades attached to a handle. It is used to cut butter or shortening into flour, which is an essential step in pastry making.

Pastry brush - Also known as a basting brush, is a cooking utensil used to spread oil or glaze on food. Traditional basting brushes are made of a plastic fiber similar to a paintbrush, while modern pastry brushes are frequently made out of silicone.

Pastry cloth - Made of canvas, a pastry cloth is used to roll out pastry. When well floured, it minimizes sticking.

Pat - To take the underside of the hand and gently press a food. The purpose might be to pat dry ingredients onto the surface so they will adhere during cooking, or to pat with a towel to remove excess moisture.

Pepper mill - A small handheld grinder containing a supply of peppercorns for grinding fresh at the table or in the kitchen.

Peppercorns - Small black, white or green dried hard berries with a pungent flavor used in almost every recipe.

Pepperoncini (pron. pep-per-awn-CHEE-nee) - Chilies that have a slightly sweet flavor that can range from medium to medium-hot. Pepperoncini are most often sold pickled and generally used as a part of antipasto and as an addition to various types of sandwiches.

Picatta - A classic Italian dish that consists of veal or chicken that has been seasoned and floured, sautéed, and served with a sauce made from the pan drippings, lemon juice, and parsley, sometimes capers are added.

Pinch - As much of an ingredient that can be held between the thumb and forefinger. A very small, approximate amount.

Pinto bean - An oval, beige-colored bean distinguished by its tan splotched surface. It is popular in Mexican dishes including chili.

Piping Bag - A conical bag with an opening for a nozzle, made of cloth and lined with plastic.

Pit - To remove the seed from a piece of fruit by cutting around the sides of the fruit and pulling the seed away from the flesh.

Pita - Pita or pitta is a round pocket bread widely consumed in many Middle Eastern and Mediterranean cuisines. It is prevalent from North Africa through the Levant and the Arabian Peninsula. The "pocket" in pita bread is created by steam, which puffs up the dough.

Pizza wheel - A pizza wheel is a round metal wheel attached to a handle. It can be rolled across pizza to cut it.

Poach - To cook food in gently simmering, never boiling, liquid.

Polenta - Coarse ground corn, as is cornmeal. Polenta makes a delicious base for sauces (ragout, mushroom, gorgonzola) and sausages; it's also good grilled or layered into lasagna-like dishes.

Pompano - This saltwater fish is a succulent, fine-textured fish with a mild delicate flavor. This expensive, moderately fat fish is considered by many experts as America's finest fish, found primarily in warmer waters of the Gulf of Mexico.

Porcelain silkscreen - A decorative process in which a special porcelain enamel is forced through a design on a screen.

Porterhouse steak - (or T-bone) The porterhouse is sometimes called the "king of all steaks" because it combines two top cuts of meat in one steak. On one side is a bone-in strip steak; the other side is the portion of the filet mignon. The porterhouse is a larger T-bone steak, with more of the tenderloin and the strip steak.

Portobello -A mushroom that is thick-fleshed with sanity caps; rich and hearty flavor. Best used for grilling, burger-style, the large, mature form of the crimini mushrooms.

Pot roast - A less-expensive cut of meat, cooked slowly in a covered pot with water, and often root vegetables and potatoes, until it is moist and tender. While any type of meat can be cooked in this way (pork or veal, for example), it is most closely associated with beef.

Potato peeler - An implement with a sharp groove and a serrated edge on one side to peel potatoes and other firm fruits and vegetables.

Pots and pans - Pots generally refer to high, straight sided cookware that will often contain larger quantities of items. Pans may refer to frying pans, cake pans or many other different types of cookware that have lower depth sides and a variety of shapes and sizes.

Preheat - To heat the oven to the specified temperature before adding the foods. Most recipes require preheating of the oven. Usually it will tell you to place in a cool oven if it should not be preheated.

Prime rib - Prime rib refers to the finest beef, with even marbling and a creamy layer of fat. It must be USDA Prime, not USDA Choice. It is generally carried only by the finest butchers. Often, rib roasts masquerade as prime rib in supermarkets, but usually carry USDA choice.

Proof - To activate yeast, or other leavening agent, before using in a recipe. The yeast is normally added to a liquid, possibly mixed with sugar, and allowed to set a given amount of time until it bubbles. If it doesn't bubble, it is old and should be discarded.

Prosciutto - Italian ham. The meat is seasoned, salt-cured, and air-dried. It is not smoked. The meat is pressed into a dense, firm texture. Parma ham is true prosciutto. Other varieties are now made in the USA.

Puff pastry - A type of crust made of a large number of successive layers of dough and butter. When baked, puff pastry becomes flaky and light (croissants for example are simply puff pastry rolls).

Pulse - An action used with processors and blenders. If a recipe tells you to pulse, turn the start button on and off rapidly several times or until the ingredients are appropriately processed.

Pumpernickel bread - Pumpernickel is a type of very heavy, slightly sweet rye bread traditionally made with coarsely ground rye. It is now often made with a combination of rye flour and whole rye berries. It has been long associated with the Westphalia region of Germany. It's very dark in color.

Punch down - To deflate a risen dough. With your hand, press on the dough until the gas escapes.

Puree - To process foods into a smooth substance of varying degrees of thickness as dictated by the recipe. Usually done with a blender, processor, sieve or food mill.

Quesadilla - A Mexican snack food made primarily of cheese inside a folded corn or wheat tortilla and cooked until the cheese melts. Occasionally a second ingredient is added with the cheese to add variety to the dish.

Quinoa (pron. KEEN-wah) - The wonder grain: high in protein, gluten-free, easy to digest, and quick to cook. Be sure to rinse it before cooking; quinoa is coated in saponin, a natural bitter-tasting insect repellent. Rinse and drain it, then cook it like pasta (in a large pot of boiling water) or rice (two parts water to one part grain). It makes a delicious breakfast (with sweet or savory additions), pilaf, and salad; it can also be added to baked goods.

Ratatouille - A vegetable stew; usually made with tomatoes, eggplant, zucchini, peppers, onion, and seasonings.

Reconstitute - To restore condensed or concentrated foods to their original strength with the addition of liquid, usually water.

Red Bean - A reddish-brown bean which can easily be mistaken for the adzuki bean, except that it has a white eye instead of a white stripe.

Reduce - To rapidly boil a liquid until it partially evaporates, leaving a thicker texture and a more intense flavor.

Refresh - To restore by placing in water. Most commonly used in reference to blanched vegetables that are placed immediately in ice water to stop the cooking, set the color and restore the crispness. Greens and herbs that are still very fresh but have gone limp can be restored to the original state by placing in cold (not ice) water and then patted dry.

Rib-eye steak - Also known as the Delmonico, Spencer, and beauty steak, this flavorful, boneless cut of prime rib (i.e., a boneless rib steak) is a favorite of steak lovers. Due to its rich marbling of fat, it is one of the most flavorful and juicy of steaks. It is also only a little less tender than the tenderloin, while adding a lot more flavorful because of the rich marbling. In its uncut form, the rib eye is known as a rib roast (prime rib)

Ribbon - Used in reference to beating a mixture, usually egg yolks and sugar, until it is thick enough to form a ribbon. Lift the beaters out of the bowl and let the excess mixture drip down into the bowl. When it forms a ribbon shape on top of the mixture in the bowl, it is ready.

Risotto - A creamy, moist, flavorsome rice dish, Italian in origin that is very, very easy to make. It does take around 20 minutes at the stove (stirring). The basis of all risotto dishes is the same, referring to the preparation of slowly adding stock or broth while constantly mixing.

Roma tomato - Roma tomato or Roma (the "Roma VF" variant is most common in seed catalogs as of 2007) is a plum tomato that is commonly found in supermarkets. The tomato is a meaty, egg- or pear-shaped tomato that is available in red and yellow. It has few seeds and is a good canning and sauce tomato.

Rosemary - Fresh or dried leaves used for lamb, poultry, soups and sauces.

Saffron - A very expensive spice with a mild and distinct flavor and used mainly in rice, poultry and seafood dishes.

Sage - Can be fresh or ground and has a pungent flavor mainly used with poultry, stuffing and pork.

Salmon - The common name for several species of fish of the family *Salmonidae*. Several other fish in the family are called trout; the difference is often said to be that salmon migrate and trout are resident, a distinction that holds true for the Salmo genus.

Salsa - Nearly any type of sauce. In American English, it usually refers to the spicy, often tomato based, hot sauces typical of Hispanic cuisine, particularly those used as dips.

Satay - A popular dish made from small pieces of meat or fish grilled on a skewer and served with a spicy peanut sauce, originating from Indonesia and Malaysia.

Sauté - Literally means "to jump." To quickly fry foods in a little fat, usually oil or butter, in an open skillet over medium-high to high heat, turning or tossing often, until tender and lightly browned, as dictated by the recipe.

Savory - A fragrant herb used with meat, poultry, fish and vegetable dishes.

Scald - To heat milk or cream to a temperature just before it boils.

Scallion - Also known as a spring onion, salad onion or green onion in many countries, scallion is an edible plant the genus *Allium*. The upper green portion is hollow. It lacks a fully developed root bulb. Harvested for their taste, they are milder than most onions.

Scallops - Edible muscle of mollusks having fan-shaped shells; served broiled or poached or in salads or cream sauces.

Score - To cut slits into foods before cooking for various purposes, including decoration, ease of cutting after cooking or tenderization. Also, the fat layer of a large cut of meat is often scored so that some of the fat melts out during roasting.

Scraper - Ideal tool for those who make their own pasta, or pastry, bread and pizza dough. Use it for cutting, cleaning and scraping the dough.

Sea bass - The lean flesh of a saltwater fish of the family *Serranidae*, any of various food and sport fishes of the Atlantic coast of the United States having an elongated body and long spiny dorsal fin.

Sear - To cook meats quickly on all sides over high heat to brown and seal in the juices. The meat should not be turned until it is well browned on each side or it will stick to the pan.

Semolina - The gritty, coarse particles of wheat left after the finer flour has passed through a bolting machine; used to make pasta.

Serrated knife - A knife with sharp, jagged notches; usually for slicing bread

Shallot - A member of the onion family shallots often have a pinkish tinge and are more delicate in flavour than some onions when cooked. Shaped like cloves of garlic.

Shred - To cut, slice or tear into thin strips. Also, to pull apart very tender cooked meats, usually with a fork.

Sieve - A tool of equal sized grooves, used for removing impurities and separating grains of different sizes. It is available in various sized grooves for different purposes.

Sift - To pass a dry ingredient through a sifter, or fine mesh screen, to loosen the particles, incorporate air, and lighten the resulting product. Also, used to combine several ingredients that are passed through at the same time.

Simmer - To cook gently just below the boiling point. If the food starts boiling, the heat is too high and should be reduced.

Sirloin steak (or top sirloin or top butt) - A multi-muscled steak cut from the sirloin section. Sirloin cuts are naturally lean and full of bold, beefy flavor. They tend to be chewier, and the most popular preparation is a quick grilling (many people marinate them first for tenderizing). The top of the sirloin contains several different cuts, all of which are called, confusingly, "sirloin steak."

Skim - To remove an undesirable substance that forms on the top surface of a liquid, usually fat, foam or scum. This is normally done by passing a flat spoon over the surface, just underneath the substance to discard. In the case of fat, if you have the time, chill the liquid first so that the fat congeals, making it very easy to remove.

Skirt steak - A boneless cut of beef from the lower part of the brisket. Cut from the beef flank, the skirt steak is the diaphragm muscle, which lies between the abdomen and chest cavity. It is a long, flat cut that is very flavorful, but tougher than most other cuts. Skirt steak has risen in popularity over the last 20 years.

Snapper - There are about 250 species of this saltwater fish, 15 of which can be found in United States waters from the Gulf of Mexico to the waters of North Carolina. Some of the better-known species include the gray snapper, mutton snapper, schoolmaster snapper and yellowtail snapper. By far the best known and most popular, however, is the red snapper, so named because of its reddish-pink skin and red eyes. Its flesh is firm textured and contains very little fat. Red snapper grows to 35 pounds but is most commonly marketed in the two- to eight-pound range. The smaller sizes are often sold whole, while larger snappers can be purchased in steaks and fillets. Snapper is available fresh all year with the peak season in the summer months. It's suitable for virtually any cooking method.

Spatula - A flat spoon of a definite shape made of plastic or rubber widely used in bakery for the purpose of mixing ingredients and for smoothening the surface.

Stainless steel - One of the two principal metals used in cookware. Extremely durable, smooth, and scratch-resistant.

Steam - A method of cooking foods over, not in, hot liquid, usually water. The heat cooks the food while the vapors keep it moist. Steaming is a good alternative to boiling because none of the nutrients or flavor is lost in the liquid. Food can also be steamed in a microwave.

Steamer - A type of cookware consisting of inserts or layers with perforations in the bottom, that are assembled together and used to cook food with the use of steam.

Steep - To soak a food in liquid for a given amount of time. Sometimes, the liquid is hot, as in tea. Other times, as with macerated fruit, the liquid is cold or room temperature.

Stew - To cook foods slowly in a specified amount of liquid in a covered pot or pan.

Stir - To move foods around with a spoon in a circular motion. Stirring is done to move foods when cooking. It is also used to cool foods after cooking. Most importantly, if a recipes calls for stirring to combine foods, such as a batter, before cooking, it usually means to gently mix just until well combined, as opposed to beating, which takes more strokes.

Stir-fry - To quickly cook foods over high or medium-high heat in a lightly oiled skillet or wok, stirring or tossing constantly, until desired or specified doneness.

Strain - To pass a liquid or moist mixture through a colander, sieve or cheese cloth to remove solid particles.

Sweat - To cook foods, usually chopped vegetables, over medium heat until they exude some of their moisture which, in turn, steams and softens the food without browning.

Tabouli (also spelled taboulleh and tabouley, among other Arabic spellings) - This is a Mediterranean salad dish, with the primary ingredients of bulgur, finely chopped parsley, mint, tomato, scallion (spring onion), and other herbs with lemon juice and various seasonings.

Tahini - A thick Middle Eastern paste made from ground sesame seeds.

Tarragon - Has a minty, licorice like flavor that is used with fish, chicken and salads.

Tartare - A preparation of finely chopped raw meat or fish optionally with seasonings and sauces.

Temper - Technically, to moderate. In cooking, tempering most often refers to slightly warming beaten eggs, by rapidly stirring a little of the hot ingredients into them, before adding them to the hot mixture so that they will combine, stirring rapidly again, without solidifying. It also refers to the softening of a heavy mixture before folding in a whipped mixture, so that incorporation occurs without deflation.

Thyme - Can be fresh or crushed leaves used in soup stocks, sauces, meats and poultry.

Timer - Many ranges, ovens and microwave ovens have built-in timers. Free-standing timers are also available.

Toast - Most commonly, to brown using a dry heat source such as an oven or toaster. However, many recipes call for toasting seeds, nuts, grains or spices before mixing with other ingredients to add flavor. They may be toasted in an oven or in a skillet, with or without oil, using a low heat, stirring or tossing often, until nicely browned, being very careful not to burn.

Tomato sauce - A leading sauce made from tomatoes, vegetables, seasonings and white stock. It may or may not be thickened with roux.

Tongs - Tongs are indispensable for turning foods, especially meat that is best not pierced with a fork.

Top-of-range - The largest segment of the cookware business, refers to products which cook by direct contact with the heat source.

Toss - To combine ingredients by gently turning over until blended. Most commonly refers to a salad, but is used for many other preparations. The easiest and most efficient way to toss is with a good pair of tongs. Alternately, two spoons, forks or one of each may be used.

Trout - Trout is a number of species of freshwater and saltwater fish belonging to the *Salmoninae* subfamily of the *Salmonidae* family. Salmon belong to some of the same genera as trout but, unlike most trout, most salmon species spend almost all their lives in salt water. Trout are classified as an oily fish.

Truss - To shape food into a desired form and secure with butcher's twine or skewers. Most commonly used with poultry or meats.

Tuna - Tuna are fish from the family *Scombridae,* mostly in the genus *Thunnus.* Tuna are fast swimmers – they have been clocked at 40 mph – and include several warm-blooded species. Unlike most fish, which have white flesh, tuna flesh is pink to dark red, which could explain their odd nickname, "rose of the sea."

Turmeric - Has a mild peppery flavor used in pickles, salads and relishes.

USDA Prime/USDA Choice - All beef is not created equal. The quality depends on not only the stock but the animal's environment, type of feed, slaughter technique, aging, butchering, packaging and other factors. The eight USDA grades are Prime, Choice, Select, Standard, Commercial, Utility, Cutter and Canner. USDA Prime is generally only available to restaurants and specialty butcher shops. The best quality sold at supermarkets is generally USDA Choice, although many markets sell only Select. If the grade is not indicated, ask. Only 2% to 3% of all beef produced is graded Prime. Prime is at its best in both flavor and texture when it is aged 18 to 24 months. About 58% of all beef produced is graded USDA

Choice. The grading is based on three factors: the proportion of meat to bone (conformation), the proportion of fat to lean (finish) and overall quality. Beef grade is largely determined by the nature of the steer, although the industry tries, through breeding and feeding practices, to raise cattle that will earn a Choice grade.

Veloute - White sauce made with stock instead of milk, either fish or chicken stock.

Vinaigrette - A mixture (emulsion) of salad oil and vinegar, often flavored with herbs, spices, and other ingredients. It is used most commonly as a salad dressing, but also as a sauce or marinade.

Whip - To beat briskly with a wire whisk or electric mixer to incorporate air, which in turn adds volume. Usually used in reference to cream or egg whites. To whip cream, which has fat, always chill the bowl, beaters and cream first. Egg whites, which are mostly water, should be whipped at room temperature.

Wild rice - Wild rice has a similar nutritional profile as grains — with twice the fiber and protein of brown rice — but is not a true grain (it's the seed of an aquatic grass). It's grown mostly in Great Lakes region, as well as California and Oregon. Some find the taste of wild rice too strong on its own and prefer to blend it with brown rice. Try it in salads, stuffings, pilafs, and side dishes, or even for breakfast.

Wire whisk - A stainless steel wire coiled to resemble a balloon, used for beating of eggs, cream etc. to incorporate air and make it lighter in texture or for blending of sauces.

Wok - Similar to a kadai, made of very thin iron metal. It enables the heat to penetrate the food items easily for faster cooking used specially in Chinese cuisine.

Zester - A zester (also, citrus zester or lemon zester) is a kitchen utensil for obtaining zest from lemons and other citrus fruit. A zester is approximately four inches long, with a handle and a curved metal end, the top of which is perforated with a row of round holes with sharpened rims.

ABOUT THE AUTHOR

From a very young age, Chef Chris De Luca has known exactly what he wants to do. His career in the kitchen started as a dishwasher for the family catering business, and as he quickly worked his way up through the ranks Chris found the fast pace, organization, hand-eye coordination, and natural palate needed to be successful in the culinary industry were all things he possessed and enjoyed using,

In 1991, at the age of 19, Chris relocated to Florida from Massachusetts. Armed with a will to learn and desire to cook, he started as a dishwasher at St. Charles Harbour, an elite yacht club residential community. His fast-rising career took him to some of Florida's most prestigious restaurants including the Grill Room at the Ritz-Carlton, Naples, a Mobil Five-Star Rating and AAA Five Diamond Award property. At the Grill, Chris was fortunate to work alongside renowned chefs including Omar Hafidi, Pierre Dousson, and the great Paul Bocuse.

Six years later Chris returned to St. Charles Harbour as executive chef, bringing with him a wealth of knowledge and skills. After three successful years at St. Charles, Chris spent the next seven years heading the kitchens of some of South Florida's finest restaurants, bringing his talent and enthusiasm for simple, refined food to his growing following. Having mastered three decades of culinary trends and forming his own concepts of food and cooking, Chris became a culinary force in the kitchens where he took the reins.

Outside the kitchen, Chris is an ISSA certified fitness trainer III and enjoys all sports. He's active in the Make-A-Wish foundation of Southern Florida, which grants the wishes of children with life-threatening conditions, and has served as a mentor in Big Brothers/Big Sisters of America.

As a chef, Chris's goal is to bring the simple techniques and pleasures of cooking to people everywhere, and especially to show single guys that this attainable skill can bring a new dynamic to the dating landscape. With his passion for great cooking and his desire to educate and entertain, Chris has become an inspiration to folks everywhere and to the women who benefit from their guy friends' newfound culinary skills.

8/13/11

239-776-0101

Eric,

Thanks so much

for the support!

Appreciate it.

Best,

Made in the USA
Charleston, SC
03 August 2011